Apress Pocket Guides

Apress Pocket Guides present concise summaries of cutting-edge developments and working practices throughout the tech industry. Shorter in length, books in this series aims to deliver quick-to-read guides that are easy to absorb, perfect for the time-poor professional.

This series covers the full spectrum of topics relevant to the modern industry, from security, AI, machine learning, cloud computing, web development, product design, to programming techniques and business topics too.

Typical topics might include:

- A concise guide to a particular topic, method, function or framework
- Professional best practices and industry trends
- A snapshot of a hot or emerging topic
- Industry case studies
- Concise presentations of core concepts suited for students and those interested in entering the tech industry
- Short reference guides outlining 'need-to-know' concepts and practices

More information about this series at `https://link.springer.com/bookseries/17385`.

Cost-Effective Graphic Solutions for Small Businesses

The Power of Visual Imaging and Design

Phillip Whitt

Apress®

Cost-Effective Graphic Solutions for Small Businesses: The Power of Visual Imaging and Design

Phillip Whitt
Columbus, GA, USA

ISBN-13 (pbk): 979-8-8688-1191-3 ISBN-13 (electronic): 979-8-8688-1192-0
https://doi.org/10.1007/979-8-8688-1192-0

Managing Director, Apress Media LLC: Welmoed Spahr
Acquisition Editors: Divya Modi, James Robinson-Prior
Coordinating Editor: Gryffin Winkler

Cover designed by eStudioCalamar

Distributed to the book trade worldwide by Apress Media, LLC, 1 New York Plaza, New York, NY 10004, U.S.A. Phone 1-800-SPRINGER, fax (201) 348-4505, e-mail orders-ny@springer-sbm.com, or visit www.springeronline.com. Apress Media, LLC is a California LLC and the sole member (owner) is Springer Science + Business Media Finance Inc (SSBM Finance Inc). SSBM Finance Inc is a **Delaware** corporation.

For information on translations, please e-mail booktranslations@springernature.com; for reprint, paperback, or audio rights, please e-mail bookpermissions@springernature.com.

Apress titles may be purchased in bulk for academic, corporate, or promotional use. eBook versions and licenses are also available for most titles. For more information, reference our Print and eBook Bulk Sales web page at http://www.apress.com/bulk-sales.

Any source code or other supplementary material referenced by the author in this book is available to readers on GitHub (https://github.com/Apress). For more detailed information, please visit https://www.apress.com/gp/services/source-code.

If disposing of this product, please recycle the paper

This book is dedicated to my loving (and patient) wife Sally. Writing a book can be a long, difficult process–she is always supportive and my biggest cheerleader.

Table of Contents

About the Author

Phillip Whitt is an author, photo retouch professional, and graphic designer. He is the author of several Apress books and video tutorials pertaining to image editing. He has edited, retouched, and restored countless digital images since the late 1990s. Phillip has served both clients from the general public and a number of commercial clients over the years. In addition to over 20 years of image editing and graphic design experience and writing about it, he is still dedicated to learning new skills. In recent years, he's earned an ExpertRating Certification in Adobe Photoshop Skills, as well as VTC certifications in GNU Image Manipulation Program (GIMP) and Scribus.

About the Technical Reviewer

Massimo Nardone is a seasoned cyber, information, and operational technology (OT) security professional with 28 years of experience working with, for example, IBM, HP, and Cognizant, with IT, OT, IoT, and IIoT security roles and responsibilities including CISO, BISO, IT/OT/IoT security architect, security assessor/auditor, PCI QSA, and ICS/SCADA expert. He is the founder of Massimo Security Services company, providing IT/OT/IoT security consulting services, and a member of ISACA, ISF, Nordic CISO Forum, and Android Global Forum, and owns four international patents. He is coauthor of five Apress IT books.

Acknowledgments

I'd like to acknowledge the team at Apress. Their support, patience, and professionalism is unparalleled.

Introduction

In today's world, there's more visual content than ever. Studies have shown that the human brain processes visual imagery far faster than text. It's imperative that small businesses position themselves to not only be visible but also stand out among the competition in the vast ocean of visual communications. Standing out doesn't always mean having the cutest or catchiest logo, tagline, or other gimmick. I believe emphasizing the quality of your product or service and placing a high value on customer service will be more meaningful in the long run.

A poster that's creative just for the sake of being creative may look good, but if it doesn't convey a clear message, it probably won't be very effective. Creativity in designing visual communications is important as long as it presents a strong, clear message that can be easily understood. Ideally, a small business can rely on its marketing department or hire a freelance designer. However, for many small businesses, that may not be feasible due to budget constraints. That's where this book comes in; it's possible for small business owners and managers to design their own compelling visuals. This book helps show the way!

The Power of Visuals in Small Business

Whether you're a small business owner, an entrepreneur, or an independent retailer, prioritizing well-designed visual communications is paramount. Your business card, flyer, or brochure must instantly capture the attention of prospective customers. By avoiding the use of hastily scribbled handwritten or poorly made signs, independent retailers can enhance their in-store presentation with professional-quality signage.

Figure 1 presents a colorful mock-up sign designed specifically for the small hardware store retail industry. Placed at the store's entrance and other key locations, it would inform customers and hopefully motivate them to shop in the paint department. This example was created using GIMP, a free image editing software program. It incorporates a high-quality stock illustration from Pexels and an AI-generated image.

Figure 1. *This mock-up design was created using the free image editor GIMP, incorporating a free stock illustration of a paint roller and an AI-generated image of several paint cans*

Overcoming Budget Constraints

Creating eye-catching graphics and designs can be expensive. Hiring a graphic designer or design firm can cost approximately from $30 to $150 per hour. Purchasing a subscription to the entire suite of applications in Adobe's Creative Cloud costs about $60 per month ($720 per year), which can add to the strain that budget-conscious small business owners are already under.

In addition to the subscription costs, there's a steep learning curve that's associated with using Adobe products. For the novice, it takes time to learn the features of each software product, as well as principles of good design. There are several free programs mentioned in this book (GIMP is one of them), and they can be an ideal solution to help keep your company's expenses down.

These programs can often complement each other, allowing you to build your own software suite. Figure 2 showcases an example of a 42-inch pull-up banner designed by Pat David, an avid open source photographer and GIMP user, for his place of employment, Dauphin Island Sea Lab. It was created using GIMP, RawTherapee (an open source program for processing RAW photographic images), and Inkscape, a free vector-drawing program that will be discussed in a later chapter.

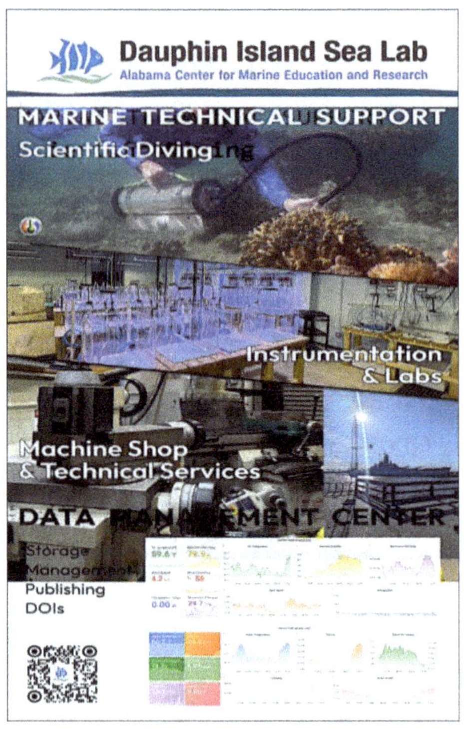

Figure 2. *This 42-inch pull-up banner was created by Pat David using three no-cost programs (image courtesy Dauphin Island Sea Lab)*

While these programs are free, there is still a learning curve to contend with. If you or one of your employees have some experience using Adobe products, the transition to the discussed alternatives should be relatively smooth. Chapter 10 explores strategies for involving employees in the creative efforts of your business.

In recent years, web-based solutions have become more prevalent—these programs offer a distinct advantage because the majority of the design work is already done. There are several browser-based programs that offer predesigned templates that can be edited to suit your business needs. Some of these programs also incorporate AI, so now it's possible to generate images and create content simply by entering a prompt.

Although these programs offer free basic features, the premium features require a paid subscription. As a general rule, the rate is about $8.00–$15.00 per month for a single user, depending on the program being utilized. This is far less expensive than a subscription to Adobe products.

One such resource is Marq (formerly Lucidpress), ideal for solopreneurs to create business cards, flyers, posters, and other marketing materials using predesigned templates (Figure 3). Marq can also accommodate small companies by offering pricing plans for teams of up to ten people, as well as larger organizations.

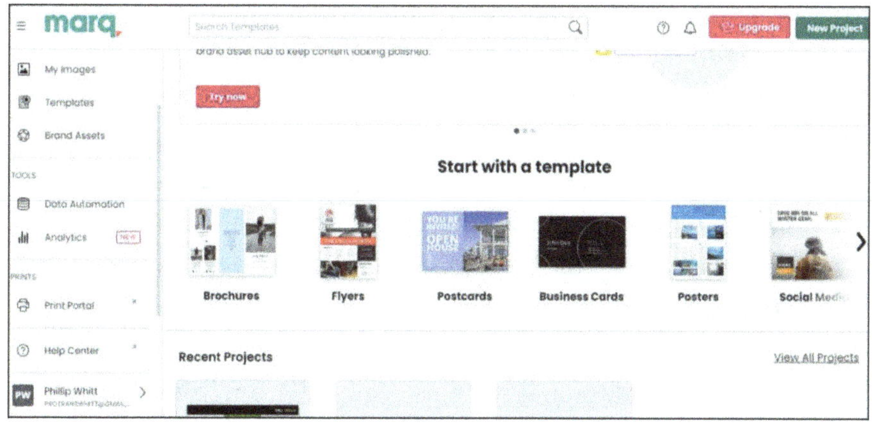

Figure 3. *Marq offers a variety of predesigned templates that make creating marketing materials easy (screenshot courtesy of Marq)*

Note It's an important consideration that there's a trade-off when creating your own visual materials as opposed to hiring a professional to handle those tasks for you. If you hire a graphic designer or design firm, they have a distinct advantage in knowledge and experience, allowing you to focus on the core tasks of your business. If hiring an outside professional is too cost prohibitive, then creating your own visuals can be a viable option. However, if you're new or inexperienced in designing visual content, it does take some time to learn. We explore strategies for you to create a "branding culture" in your organization and involving employees in the creative process.

Empowering Small Businesses with Graphic Solutions

I've written this book, *Cost-Effective Graphic Solutions for Small Businesses,* to be your guide to creating engaging visual content without breaking the bank.

We'll explore a number of free and budget-friendly graphic resources that will enable you to create stunning, effective visual communications.

We'll also explore some basic design principles to help you create professional quality work that represents your business in the best light.

This book is a treasure trove of valuable insights and practical tips. Whether you are a solopreneur or part of a small team, you'll discover creative solutions to enhance your marketing materials, social media presence, and overall brand image.

Note You may also be interested in my book *Pro Freeware and Open Source Solutions for Business* (now in its second edition). While it covers some of the same software discussed in this book to a far lesser degree, it is a reference for all types of free and low-cost software for office productivity, point-of-sale, project management, and more.

Let this book be your go-to guide in the search for affordable graphic resources that will help you create visual content that makes an impact. As we get underway, I hope this content helps you find the graphic resources and solutions to help your small business thrive and stand out in a crowded market.

If you're ready to get started, let's move on to Chapter 1.

PART I

Foundations for Effective Visuals

CHAPTER 1

Getting Started

If you're ready to dive into the basics of creating compelling visuals, let's get started! This chapter will get things underway by exploring these key areas:

- Understanding the significance of visual content in business
- Basic design principles
    - Balance
    - Alignment
    - Contrast
    - Typography
- Summary

Understanding the Significance of Visual Content in Business

In this modern age of high-speed Internet, social media, and other types of digital communication (as well as printed), the impact of visual content is crucial for any business to stand out and compete. Society's attention span seems to be much shorter these days, so your image-oriented marketing materials must capture the prospect's attention immediately.

P. Whitt, *Cost-Effective Graphic Solutions for Small Businesses*, Apress Pocket Guides, https://doi.org/10.1007/979-8-8688-1192-0_1

Any small business operating on a budget can benefit from this book—particularly those involved in independent retailing. Drawing on my experience as a former advertising manager in a retail home center, one of my pet peeves is poorly made handwritten signs. Not only do they diminish the company's professional image, but they can also lead to frustrated customers when signs are difficult to read, contain glaring grammatical errors, or convey a confusing message.

Figure 1-1 shows a real-life example of a handwritten sign on the left (notice the word *Globes* is hard to make out). The right-hand example is a mock-up that was created using an AI-generated image and the image editing program GIMP.

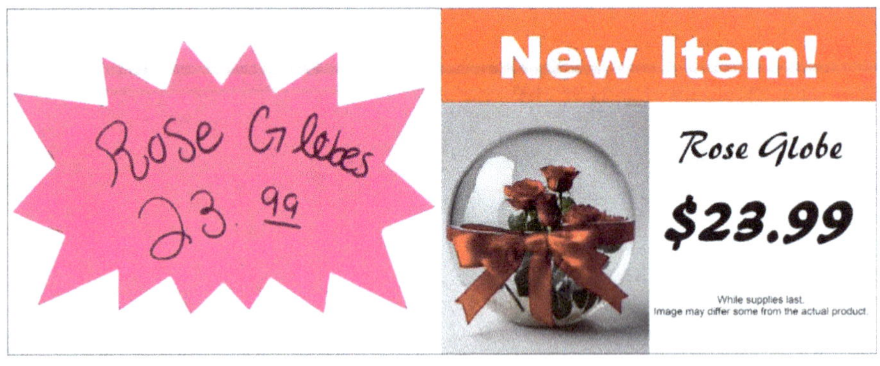

Figure 1-1. *A handwritten sign compared to one designed using GIMP and an AI-generated image*

Note Before utilizing AI-generated images, I suggest you read the service provider's license agreement. In the previous example, the image of the rose globe was generated using Pixlr, and according to the terms of use, Pixlr reserves the right to use it any way they deem fit but grants the user the right to use the output image for any purpose (personal or commercial). The license agreement be accessed here: `https://pixlr.com/ai-generator-license/`.

There are some exceptions that can be made to banning the use of handwritten signs. In some cases, handwritten signs may be appropriate for less formal markets (such as a farmer's market or the produce section of a small town grocer). Figure 1-2 shows an example of a well-crafted sign.

Figure 1-2. *A well-crafted handmade sign*

When we think about visual communications, it's usually in a marketing sense, intended to encourage prospective customers to purchase the product or service being marketed. Nevertheless, effective design can also encompass other facets of communicating with the public, such as conveying store policies.

For instance, Figure 1-3 presents a side-by-side comparison of a handwritten notice from a local grocer alongside an enhanced version created using a computer (using the free program GIMP). Notice that the computer-generated version not only improves the visual appeal but also clarifies the message.

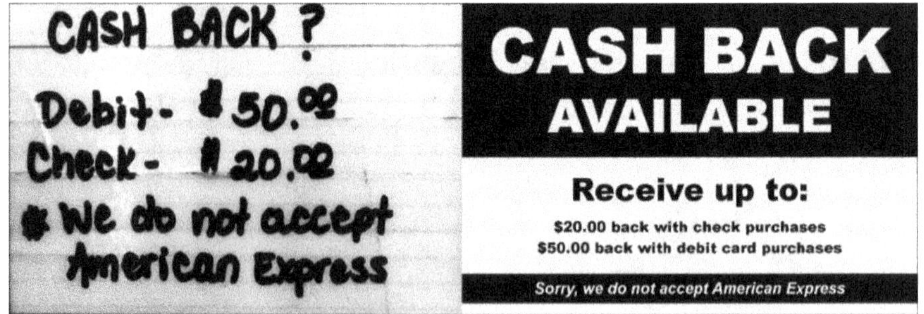

Figure 1-3. *A comparison of a handprinted notice and a more visually appealing, computer-created version*

Basic Design Principles

I should mention that this book primarily serves as an introduction to cost-effective resources to crafting your own visual designs; it's not a comprehensive design course. However, we'll go over a few fundamental principles of design in this chapter. In the following chapter, you'll find a step-by-step tutorial on designing a flyer using Paint.NET, offering valuable basic training.

In this section, we'll look at the following: *balance, alignment, contrast,* and *typefaces.*

Balance

When crafting your designs, an important consideration is ensuring that elements are evenly distributed to achieve visual stability. Balance can be attained through symmetrical or asymmetrical arrangements.

In Figure 1-4, a side-by-side comparison is presented, featuring the original real-life sign (with the logo replaced by a fictitious version) juxtaposed with a redesigned, more visually balanced version. The original version appears top-heavy (note the large amount of whitespace in the bottom portion). In the revised version, the elements are distributed more evenly, giving the design more balance. Also, the revised version is a little more informative; it provides a general description of the type of applicants the company desires, a financial incentive for applying, and a clear call to action.

Figure 1-4. *The side-by-side comparison of the original sign and the redesigned version*

Alignment

Maintaining consistent alignment of text, images, and other elements helps to create a clean, organized layout. In the example shown in Figure 1-5, the elements are center aligned (which also helps make this design well balanced).

Figure 1-5. *The elements in this design are center aligned*

It's important to keep in mind that designs should include relevant information and graphic elements but should not include extraneous content that makes it appear busy or crowded.

In text documents, the content is usually justified left (meaning the text is anchored to the left margin of the document). Text can be justified *left, right, center,* or *filled,* as shown in Figure 1-6.

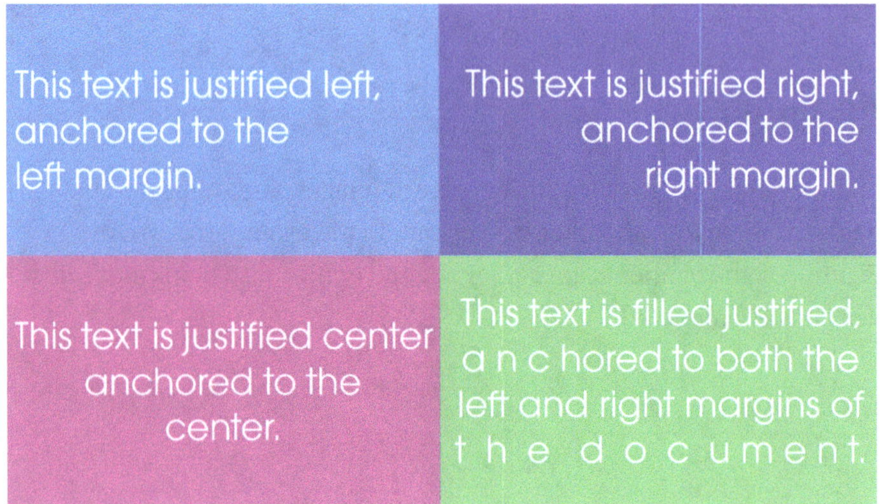

Figure 1-6. *An example of text justified left, right, center, and filled*

Justifying text helps in placement of graphic elements in your visual designs.

Contrast

Contrast can be an effective way to capture attention. One way of doing this is by using contrasting colors. Figure 1-7 shows a color wheel, each color's opposite directly across on the other side of the wheel.

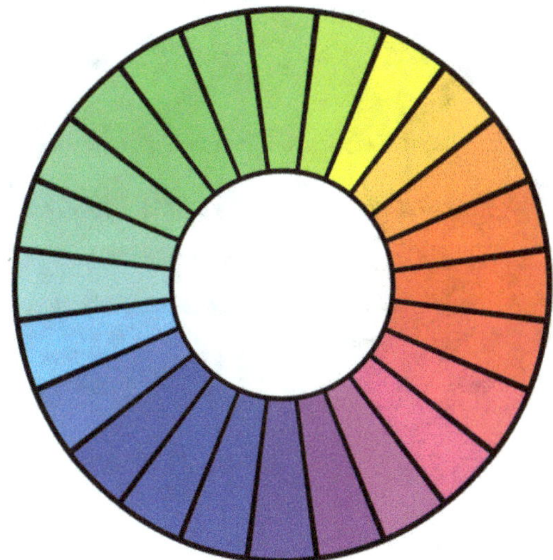

Figure 1-7. *A color wheel is useful for determining contrasting colors*

In the following example, opposing green and purple hues are used in this flyer for a fictional bicycle company (Figure 1-8).

Figure 1-8. *Opposing green and purple hues add attention-grabbing contrast*

In the following example, opposing green and purple hues are used in this flyer for a fictional bicycle company (Figure 1-8).

Contrast can be achieved by using juxtaposing themes and using different typefaces. Figure 1-9 shows an example of a cityscape split into day and night versions. Note the difference in the typefaces; the first is more formal, while the second is more informal and whimsical.

Figure 1-9. *An example of achieving contrast by splitting the cityscape into day and night versions and utilizing different typefaces*

Typography

This is a very important topic in creating visual designs. This is a subject that is beyond the scope of this book to cover in depth, but the following should give you an idea how to use certain fonts for specific purposes. Figure 1-10 shows several different typefaces.

Figure 1-10. *A variety of different typefaces*

Here's a description of the typeface characteristics and how they can potentially be used.

Based on the image you provided, here are the characteristics and potential applications of each typeface:

1. Academy Engraved

   Characteristics: A delicate, formal Sans-serif typeface with an engraved, elegant appearance. It uses thin lines with subtle variations in stroke width.

   Potential Applications: Suitable for formal invitations, announcements, certificates, and headings where a refined, sophisticated appearance is required.

2. Amazone BT

   Characteristics: This typeface has a curved, flowing appearance. With a handwritten quality, it projects a more personal and intimate feel.

   Potential Applications: Ideal for wedding or dinner party invitations, greeting cards, and branding for companies with the need to convey elegance and personal touch, such as florists, boutique shops, and bridal shops.

3. Avignon Pro

   Characteristics: A Sans-serif typeface with a clean, modern appearance. It utilizes geometric structure and uniform stroke widths.

   Potential Applications: Ideal for body text in print or web, signage, and digital media where readability is a priority. It works well in minimalist and contemporary design and can be used for a variety of purposes.

4. Blackoak Std

   Characteristics: A bold, heavy display typeface with thick, blocky letters; it implies a strong presence.

   Potential Applications: A good choice for use in headlines, posters, or any design where grabbing viewer attention is the important. Suitable for sports, adventure, or action-oriented themes.

5. Giddyup Std

   Characteristics: A whimsical, hand-drawn script with playful curves and loops. It has a casual, fun appearance.

   Potential Applications: Perfect for children's books, western themes, playful branding, greeting cards, or informal event invitations where a sense of fun and light-hardheartedness is desired.

6. John Handy LET

   Characteristics: A brush script font that imitates natural handwriting with a casual, artistic flair. It has uneven strokes that convey a relaxed, handmade quality.

   Potential Applications: Great for creative branding, logos, artistic event invitations, or any design that requires a personalized, artisan feel.

7. Arial

   Characteristics: A widely used Sans-serif typeface with simple, clean lines and good readability at small sizes. It has a neutral, modern appearance.

   Potential Applications: Suitable for body text in documents, websites, and presentations. Often used in professional and corporate settings due to its clarity and versatility.

8. Stencil BT

   Characteristics: A bold typeface with a stencil-like design, characterized by breaks in the strokes that mimic the style used in stenciling.

   Potential Applications: Ideal for military-themed designs, industrial signage, packaging, and any context where a rugged, utilitarian look is desired.

9. Times New Roman

   Characteristics: A serif typeface with a classic, traditional look. It has a moderate stroke contrast and is highly readable.

   Potential Applications: Commonly used in newspapers, books, academic papers, and formal documents due to its readability and professional appearance.

10. Wedding Text BT

    Characteristics: A decorative, ornate script with a highly formal, calligraphic style. It features intricate loops and flourishes.

    Potential Applications: Best suited for wedding invitations, formal event programs, certificates, and other elegant, formal occasions where a touch of sophistication is needed.

Summary

This chapter provided a glimpse of how important visual communications are in business. It also provided a few tips on design basics. Here's what we covered:

- Understanding the significance of visual content in business
- Basic design principles
    - Balance
    - Alignment
    - Contrast
    - Typography

In the next chapter, we'll discuss the free Windows-based image editing program Paint.NET. It includes a tutorial on designing a marketing piece to help you get better acquainted with this application.

PART II

No-Cost Software Titles

CHAPTER 2

Paint.NET: The Free Image Editor for Windows

This chapter provides a brief overview of Paint.NET. This is a free, Windows-based image editing program that's easy for new users to learn. The key features we'll look at are:

- An introduction to Paint.NET
- Basic features and functions
    - The toolbar
    - Adjustments
    - Effects
    - Layers
- Increasing functionality with plug-ins
- Designing a business card with Paint.NET
- Summary

P. Whitt, *Cost-Effective Graphic Solutions for Small Businesses*, Apress Pocket Guides,
https://doi.org/10.1007/979-8-8688-1192-0_2

An Introduction to Paint.NET

Paint.NET is a free, Windows-based image editing program. It's similar to Adobe Photoshop but is a lighter program without the high-end features. It's a useful tool for editing or retouching photographic images, which can be handy for preparing images to use in marketing materials or other visual communications. Paint.NET was used to digitally remove the power lines in the image shown in Figure 2-1.

***Figure 2-1.** Before-and-after comparison*

Paint.NET can also be used to create original raster (bitmapped) artwork. The illustration shown in Figure 2-2 was created using Paint.NET.

Figure 2-2. *This illustration was created using Paint.NET*

For a no-cost application, Paint.NET is surprisingly capable. It can be enhanced with the addition of plug-ins (which we'll take a closer look a little later in this chapter).

Paint.NET can be downloaded from the official website at `https://www.getpaint.net/index.html`.

Paint.NET is a capable yet lightweight program with a variety of strengths and weaknesses. Here's a list of Paint.NET's pros and cons:

Pros

- Free to download and use for personal or commercial purposes.
- Features a simple, intuitive interface that's easy to learn.
- Layer-based.

- Unlimited history allows the user to go back to an earlier point in the editing session to correct mistakes.
- User license permits installation on as many computers as needed.
- Supports a variety of popular file formats.

Cons

- Only works on Windows (version 10 or later).
- Lacks the more advanced features found in Adobe Photoshop or GIMP (although its capabilities can be enhanced by adding plug-ins).
- Text tool is a bit lacking in functionality.

Basic Features and Functions

If you're familiar with Adobe Photoshop, you'll notice that the interface of Paint.NET (Figure 2-3) shares many similarities but with fewer tools and features.

Figure 2-3. *The Paint.NET interface*

The interface is customizable to suit the user's preferences, including the color scheme which can be set to blue, light, or dark.

While it's beyond the scope of this book to offer a detailed analysis of the program, it does highlight some important areas worth noting. If you're new to Paint.NET, I recommend taking some time to read through the documentation found here: `https://www.getpaint.net/doc/latest/index.html`.

Note If you'd like to learn this program in greater depth, you find my book *Practical Paint.NET*, available from Apress, of interest. For more information, simply visit `https://link.springer.com/book/10.1007/978-1-4842-7283-1`.

The Toolbar

The Paint.NET toolbar offers a wide assortment of tools designed for editing layers, pixels, selecting portions of an image, application of colors, gradients, and text, along with a variety of other editing functions to enhance your images. Figure 2-4 shows an example of using the Clone tool to touch up a small area of the image.

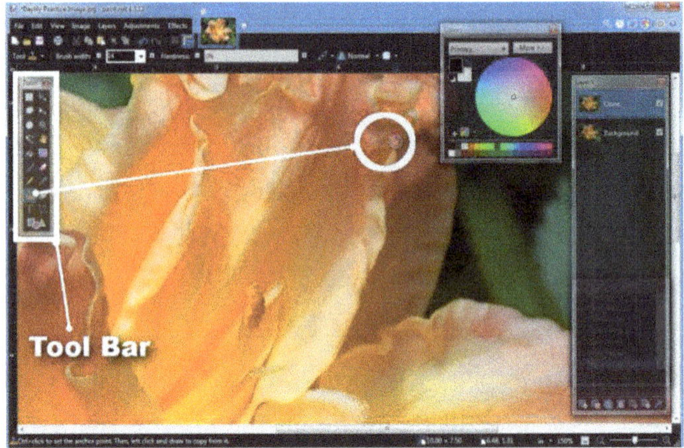

Figure 2-4. *Touching up a small area using the Clone tool*

Adjustments

The Adjustments Menu contains the functions for making tonal and color adjustments. It contains a number of dialogs for correcting brightness, contrast, and color. Figure 2-5 illustrates an example of boosting the color saturation of the image using the Hue/Saturation dialog.

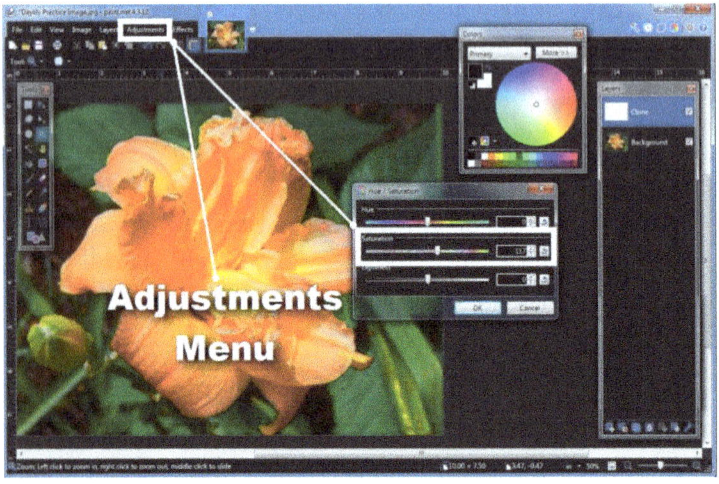

Figure 2-5. *Boosting the color saturation using the Hue/ Saturation dialog*

Effects

The Effects menu contains the functions for adding artistic and other special effects to the image. Figure 2-6 shows the Ink Sketch filter applied to the image.

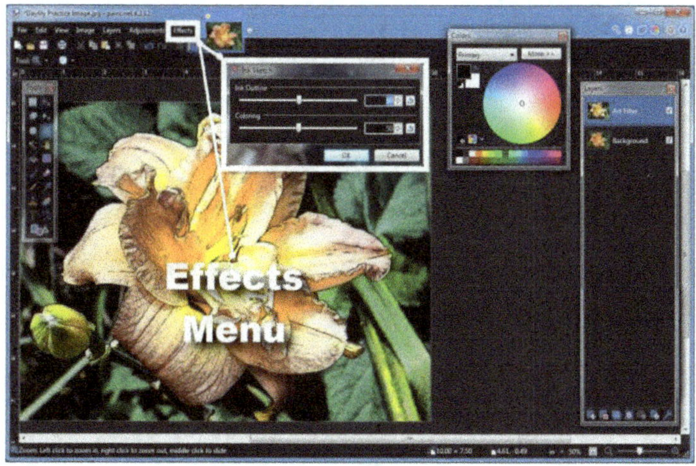

Figure 2-6. *The Ink Sketch filter dialog*

Layers

Layers can be thought of as a series of transparent acetate sheets, each one containing a graphic element. When combined, they result in a complete image. This is a useful aspect of image editing because revisions can be performed on individual layers, preserving the rest of the image and preventing the need to reedit the entire work from scratch.

Figure 2-7 shows an example of a flyer created in Paint.NET, with each graphical element on its own layer.

Figure 2-7. *An example of a flyer created in Paint.NET, with each graphical element on its own layer*

Increasing Functionality with Plug-ins

Paint.NET's capabilities can be expanded by installing software components known as plug-ins. These valuable tools are created and shared by members of the Paint.NET community. To learn more about plug-ins, the *Installing Additional Plugins* page within the Paint.NET documentation is a good place to start. You can find a detailed guidance on this in Figure 2-8: `https://www.getpaint.net/doc/latest/InstallPlugins.html](https://www.getpaint.net/doc/latest/InstallPlugins.html)`.

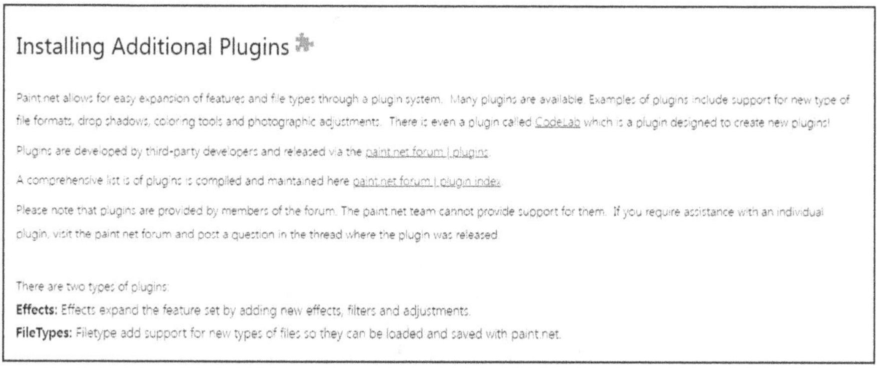

Installing Additional Plugins

Paint.net allows for easy expansion of features and file types through a plugin system. Many plugins are available. Examples of plugins include support for new type of file formats, drop shadows, coloring tools and photographic adjustments. There is even a plugin called CodeLab which is a plugin designed to create new plugins!

Plugins are developed by third-party developers and released via the paint.net forum | plugins.

A comprehensive list is of plugins is compiled and maintained here paint.net forum | plugin index.

Please note that plugins are provided by members of the forum. The paint.net team cannot provide support for them. If you require assistance with an individual plugin, visit the paint.net forum and post a question in the thread where the plugin was released.

There are two types of plugins:

Effects: Effects expand the feature set by adding new effects, filters and adjustments.

FileTypes: Filetype add support for new types of files so they can be loaded and saved with paint.net.

Figure 2-8. *The Installing Additional Plugins page in the Paint.NET documentation*

EXERCISE: CREATING A BUSINESS CARD IN PAINT.NET

If you're a Windows user and would like to attempt this exercise (after first downloading and installing Paint.NET), it will provide you with some hands-on experience and help you become familiar with the program.

In this exercise, we'll create a business card for a (fictional) newly opened bicycle company called *Midtown Cycles* (any relation to any actual companies with that name is coincidental), whose owner is on a shoestring budget but needs to save as much cash as possible. Utilizing Paint.NET rather than buying a software subscription is one way to achieve this.

Now, if you feel inclined, let's give this exercise a try. *If the specific fonts the exercise calls for are not installed on your system, simply substitute the closest one available.*

1. Launch Paint.NET.
2. From the menu at the top left corner of the interface, open a new file (File ➤ New), or use the keyboard shortcut Ctrl+New—the *New* dialog will launch.

3. In the dialog under the *Pixel size* settings, set the Resolution to 300 pixels/inch; under the *Print size* settings, set the Width to 3.5 inches and the Height to 2 inches as shown in Figure 2-9, then click OK.

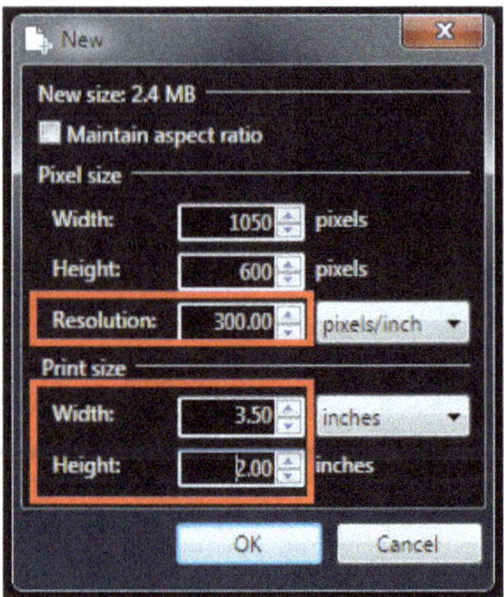

Figure 2-9. *Set the resolution to 300, width 3.5 inches, and height 2 inches*

4. Add a new layer (Layers ➤ Add New Layer), or use the keyboard shortcut Ctrl+Shift+New.

5. Double-click the new layer's preview thumbnail to open the Layer Properties dialog; rename the layer *Light Gray Background* (Figure 2-10).

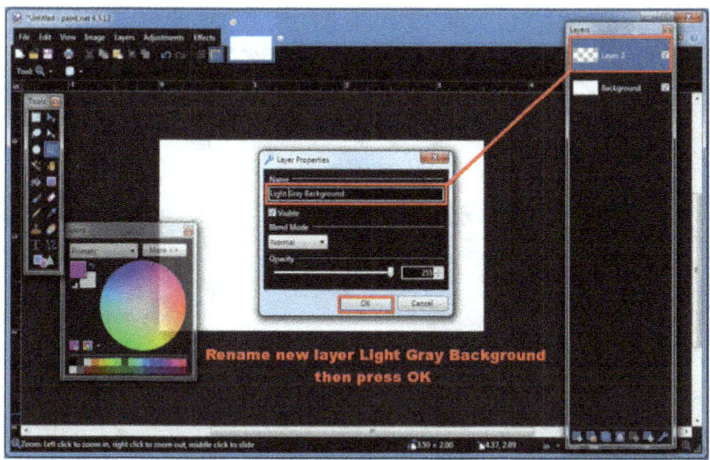

Figure 2-10. *Rename the new layer Light Gray Background*

6. Open the Colors menu (F8); click *More* to expand the window.
7. Set the Primary color to a light gray using these RGB values shown in Figure 2-11:
   - **Red**: 215
   - **Green**: 215
   - **Blue**: 215

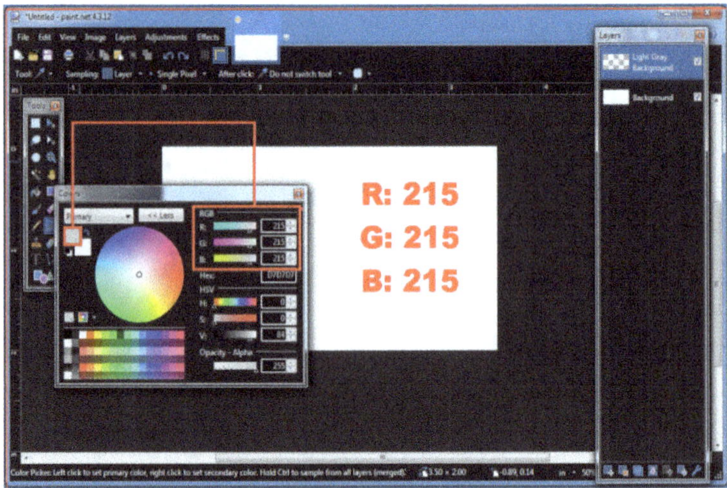

Figure 2-11. *Set the Primary color to a light gray using the RGB values as shown*

8. Click the Paint Bucket tool icon, or click F.
9. Click in the design to fill the layer with light gray.
10. Add a new layer (Layers ➤ Add New Layer), or use the keyboard shortcut Ctrl+Shift+New.
11. Double-click the new layer's preview thumbnail to open the Layer Properties dialog; rename the layer *Midtown* (a line of text will be placed in this layer).
12. Click the *Text* tool icon (or click T); choose *Avignon Pro Demi* as the font, set the size to 22 points—type *Midtown* as one word in the center of the workspace.
13. Use the *Move Selected Pixels* tool (M) to position the text as shown (Figure 2-12); there should be about 1/4" of space at the top of the text and at the top edge and 9/16" from the right-hand side edge—deactivate the selection (Ctrl+D) after the text is positioned.

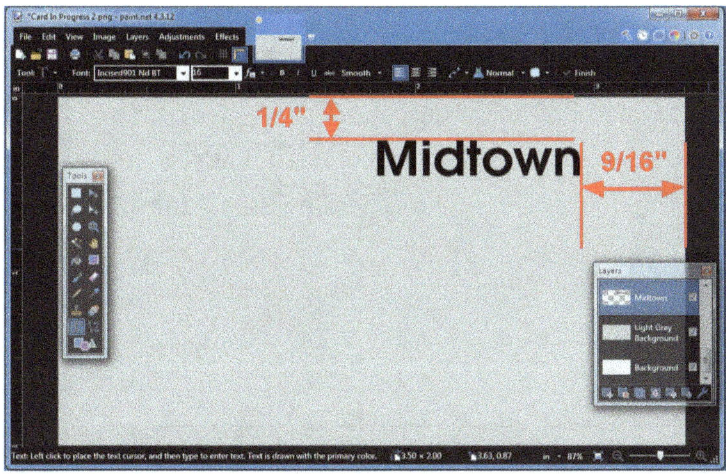

Figure 2-12. *Use the Move Selected Pixels tool to position the text as shown*

14. Add a new layer (Layers ➤ Add New Layer), or use the keyboard shortcut Ctrl+Shift+New.

15. Double-click the new layer's preview thumbnail to open the Layer Properties dialog; rename the layer *Cycle Shop* (a line of text will be placed in this layer).

16. Click the *Text* tool icon (or click T); choose *Incised 901 Nd BT* as the font, and set the size to 16 points—type *Cycle Shop* as two words in the center of the workspace.

17. Use the *Move Selected Pixels* tool (M) to position the text as shown (Figure 2-13); there should be about 1/8" of space between this text and the line that reads Midtown; the last character of this text should be about ¼" from the right edge of the card—deactivate the selection (Ctrl+D) after positioned.

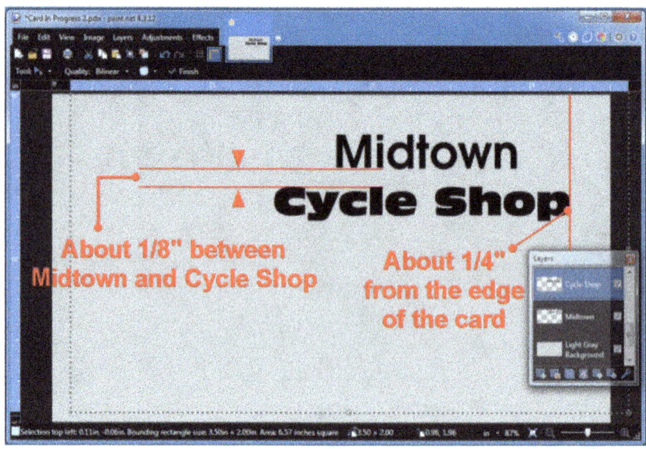

***Figure 2-13.** Use the Move Selected Pixels tool to position the text as shown*

18. Next, we'll put a small graphic of a bicycle in place; to obtain the graphic, follow this link to OpenClipArt.org: `https://openclipart.org/detail/243022/detailed-bicycle-silhouette`.

19. After the page loads, right-click the image of the BMX bike, and then select Copy image (Figure 2-14).

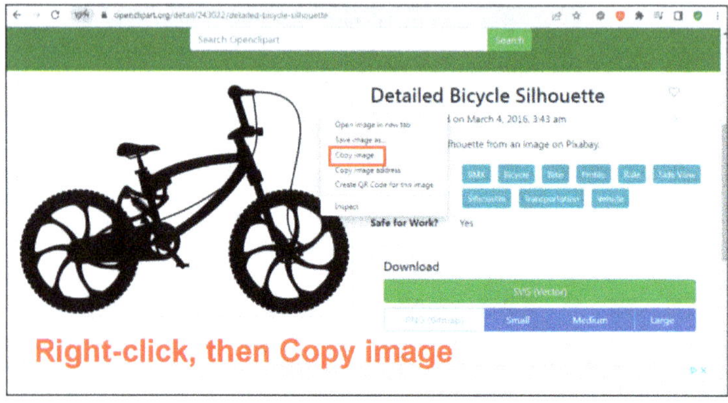

***Figure 2-14.** Right-click, then copy image*

20. The image is now contained in the program's clipboard; paste it into a new layer (Edit ➤ Paste into New Layer).

21. Double-click the new layer's preview thumbnail to open the Layer Properties dialog; rename the layer *Bike* (Figure 2-15).

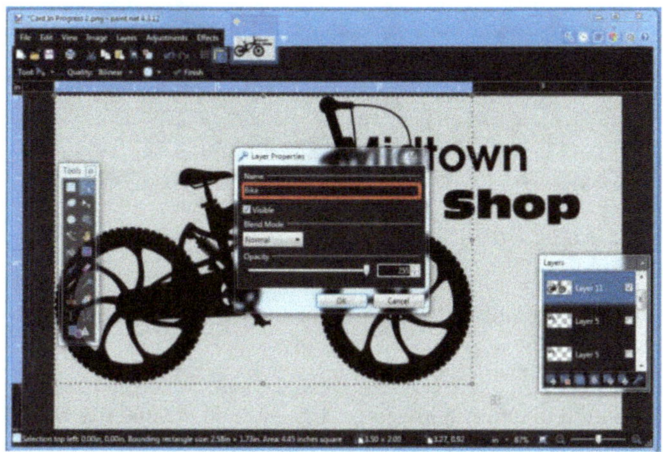

Figure 2-15. *Rename the new layer Bike*

22. Click the *Move Selected Pixels* tool icon (or click M); hold the shift key, and click the lower right corner of the bike graphic.

23. Reduce the size until it's about 1–1/8" long; move into position as shown in Figure 2-16. It should be about 1/8" from the left edge and about 7/8" from the top edge to the bottom of the graphic.

Figure 2-16. *Position the graphic as shown*

24. Deselect the graphic (Edit ➤ Deselect), or use the keyboard shortcut Ctrl+D.
25. Open the Colors window (F8); click *More* to expand the window.
26. Set the Primary color to a green hue using these values:

    R: 155

    G: 255

    B: 18
27. Add a new layer (Layers ➤ Add New Layer), or use the keyboard shortcut Ctrl+Shift+New.
28. Double-click the new layer's preview thumbnail to open the Layer Properties dialog; rename the layer *Green Box.*
29. Using the *Rectangle Select* tool (S), draw a selection in the lower portion of the design as shown in Figure 2-17, leaving just a little space under the graphic image.

Figure 2-17. *Make a rectangular selection in the design as shown*

30. Use the *Paint Bucket* tool (F) to fill the selected area with the active color, and then deactivate the selection (Ctrl+D).

31. Open the Colors window (F8); click *More* to expand the window.

32. Set the Primary color to a purple hue using these values:

    R: 178

    G: 0

    B: 255

33. Add a new layer (Layers ➤ Add New Layer), or use the keyboard shortcut Ctrl+Shift+New.

34. Double-click the new layer's preview thumbnail to open the Layer Properties dialog; rename the layer *Purple Stripe.*

35. Using the *Rectangle Select* tool (S), draw a selection about ¾" high, with the top edge just under the graphic as shown in Figure 2-18.

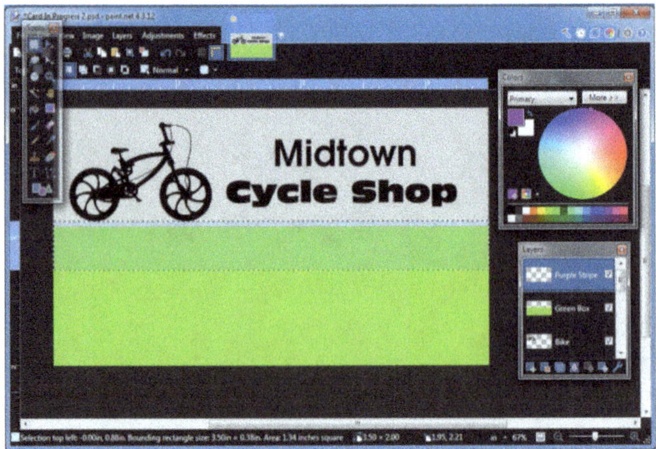

Figure 2-18. *Make a rectangular selection in the design as shown*

36. Use the *Paint Bucket* tool (F) to fill the selected area with the active color, and then deactivate the selection (Ctrl+D).
37. Add a new layer (Layers ➤ Add New Layer), or use the keyboard shortcut Ctrl+Shift+New.
38. Double-click the new layer's preview thumbnail to open the Layer Properties dialog; rename the layer *Glenn Howard-Owner* (this is just a fictional owner's name).
39. Open the Colors menu (F8); choose *white* as the Primary color.
40. Click the *Text* tool icon (or click T); choose *Avignon Pro* as the font, set the size to 10 points, and the *Center Align* option is selected—type *Glenn Howard*, click the spacebar, the *Owner* next line.
41. Use the *Move Selected Pixels* tool (M) to position the text in the center as shown (Figure 2-19).

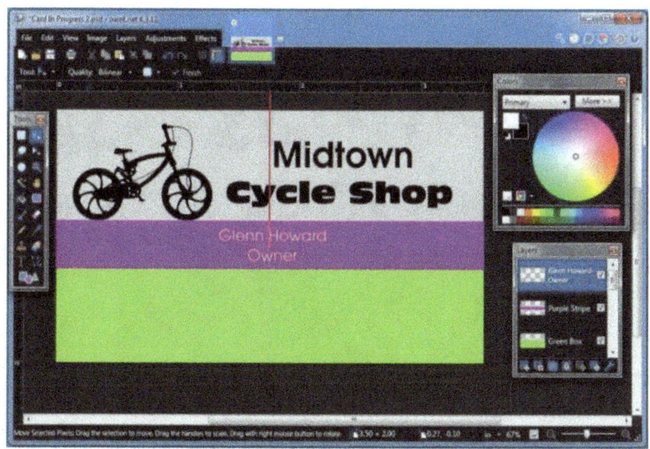

Figure 2-19. *Position the text in the center as shown*

42. Add a new layer (Layers ➤ Add New Layer), or use the keyboard shortcut Ctrl+Shift+New.
43. Double-click the new layer's preview thumbnail to open the Layer Properties dialog; rename the layer *Contact Information.*
44. Open the Colors menu (F8); choose *black* as the Primary color.
45. Click the *Text* tool icon (or click T); choose *Avignon Pro* as the font, set the size to 8 points, and the *Align Left* option is selected.
46. Type *1234 Maple Lane* in the lower left area shown in Figure 2-20; hold the *spacebar* down until the cursor is in the position indicated by the arrow.

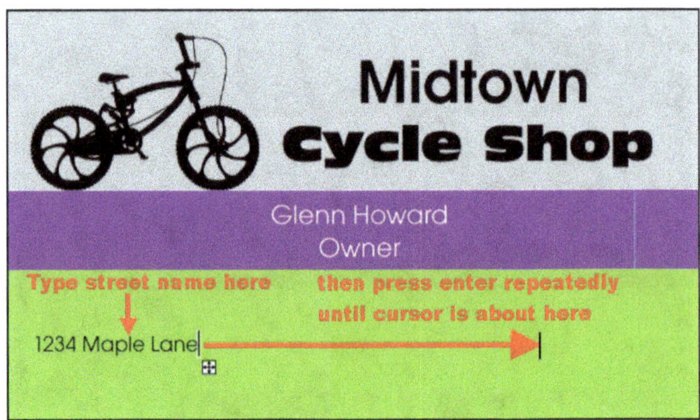

***Figure 2-20.** Position the text in the lower left area, and then hold the spacebar down until the cursor is in the position indicated by the arrow*

47. Type *123-456-7890* (a fictitious phone number) in the lower right area shown in Figure 2-21; click just past the 0; place the cursor where it's indicated by the arrow.

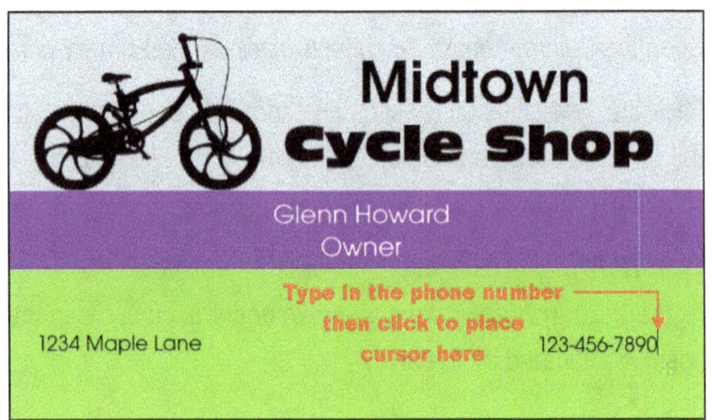

***Figure 2-21.** After typing the number, click just past the 0 ; place the cursor as indicated by the arrow*

48. Click the Enter (Return) key to start a new line indicated in Figure 2-22.

Figure 2-22. *Click the Enter (Return) key to start a new line indicated by the arrow*

49. Type *Anytown, USA*, then hold the spacebar down to advance the cursor to the area indicated in Figure 2-23. Type `www.web.com` as placeholder text.

Figure 2-23. *Advance the cursor to the point shown, and then type the text as shown*

This exercise is now complete. When making actual marketing materials, make sure the elements (such as text, graphics, etc.) are positioned correctly (there are tips online that can help with this). When creating visual materials using Paint.NET, be sure to save a layered version in the native PDN format. A flattened JPEG version can be used in a business card template and then printed using a color inkjet or laser printer (Figure 2-24).

Figure 2-24. *Business card designs can be placed into templates then printed*

If you opt to print your own marketing materials, you can purchase prescored business card stock (as well as paper stock for brochures and flyers) from office supply stores or online. The corresponding template can usually be downloaded from the manufacturer's website.

Summary

Here's a brief recap of what was covered in this chapter:

- An introduction to Paint.NET (including the pros and cons)
- Basic features and functions (this briefly covered the toolbar, adjustments, effects, and layers)
- Increasing functionality with plug-ins
- Designing a business card with Paint.NET

If you'd like more practice using Paint.NET, then visit the Beginner Tutorials page found here: `https://forums.getpaint.net/forum/20-beginner-tutorials/`.

In the next chapter, we'll explore the free editing program GIMP.

CHAPTER 3

GIMP: A Powerful Free Alternative to Photoshop

This chapter explores the free and open source program GIMP (GNU Image Manipulation Program), a free alternative to Adobe Photoshop. Although similar to Paint.NET, GIMP is also more powerful and complex—thus capable of advanced raster illustration and image editing. Here are the aspects of GIMP we'll touch on:

- An introduction to GIMP
- The GIMP workspace
    - Menus
    - Tools and tool settings
    - Layers
- GIMP tutorials
- Summary

P. Whitt, *Cost-Effective Graphic Solutions for Small Businesses*, Apress Pocket Guides,
https://doi.org/10.1007/979-8-8688-1192-0_3

An Introduction to GIMP

GIMP (which is an acronym for *GNU Image Manipulation Program*) is a popular alternative to Adobe Photoshop. GIMP is primarily a tool for both basic and advanced photo editing. While Paint.NET can handle a wide range of photo editing tasks, GIMP has many features for more advanced image editing.

Although GIMP and Paint.NET are similar in many ways, there are some significant differences between the two programs. These differences can be advantages or disadvantages, depending on the user's needs. For example, GIMP is a cross-platform program, capable of running on Windows, macOS, and Linux (Paint.NET is limited to Windows-based computers). Paint.NET offers a basic tool set, allowing new users to quickly get up and running. GIMP offers a much broader tool set for advanced editing, but may be overwhelming for new users to learn.

As an example of GIMP's advanced editing abilities, Figure 3-1 depicts a before-and-after comparison of a 1950s era photo in black and white, followed by a colorized version.

Figure 3-1. *A 1950s era photograph that was colorized using GIMP. (Image courtesy of Bruce Bundt)*

GIMP is also useful for raster image creation and illustration. Figure 3-2 shows a rendering of a night cityscape created using GIMP.

Figure 3-2. *An illustration of a cityscape created using GIMP (image copyright 2021 Phillip Whitt)*

GIMP can be a useful tool for creating visual content for your business. Figure 3-3 demonstrates how GIMP was used to create a mock-up of a 16" × 20" window poster for a hypothetical shop specializing in vintage records, tapes, and other collectibles. The graphical elements (free to use in personal or commercial work) were obtained from OpenClipArt.org and incorporated into the design.

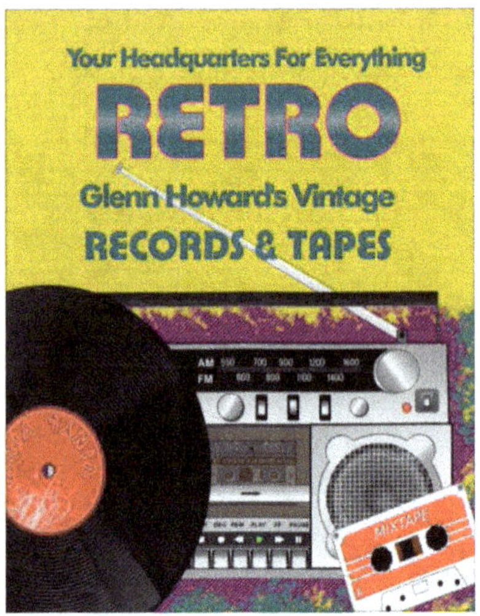

Figure 3-3. *GIMP was used to create this mock-up of a window poster*

GIMP is a free, open source program that can be installed on an unlimited number of computers—if your company expands, you can install GIMP on added computers without having to pay additional license fees (as you would with proprietary software).

It can also be distributed freely, so there's no need to worry about raising legal issues, pirating, or unlawful distribution (provided it's done under the terms of the *GNU General Public License*). For those with coding experience, you can even modify the source code to suit your specific needs, according to the terms of the GPL. You can learn more about the GPL terms here: `https://www.gimp.org/about/COPYING`.

Unlike Paint.NET, which can only be used on Windows, GIMP can be installed on MacOS, Linux, FreeBSD, as well as Windows.

As powerful and capable as GIMP is, it does have some downsides that we'll explore shortly. Here's a list of GIMP's pros and cons:

Pros

- Free to download and use for personal or commercial purposes; can be installed on as many computers as needed.
- Can be freely copied and distributed according to the terms of the General Public License.
- A powerful editor that can serve as a viable alternative to Adobe Photoshop in many cases.
- Layer-based.
- Utilizes layer masks for advanced selection techniques.
- Supports a wide variety of popular file formats.
- Can be installed on Windows, MacOS, and Linux.

Cons

- Can be difficult for new users to learn.
- Only offers partial compatibility with Adobe Photoshop.
- GIMP is updated sporadically; in their defense, GIMP is developed and maintained by volunteers with regular jobs, so they must update GIMP as time allows.

To download GIMP, simply visit the downloads page here: `https://www.gimp.org/downloads/`.

The GIMP Workspace

After GIMP has been downloaded and installed, it can then be launched. It usually takes a few minutes for this process to complete. By default, GIMP launches in the *Single-Window Mode* as shown in Figure 3-4.

***Figure 3-4.** The GIMP workspace in the default Single-Window Mode*

If you prefer to work with floating panels that can be moved (like those in Paint.NET), the Single-Window mode can be switched off (Windows ➤ Single-Window Mode). Figure 3-5 shows the GIMP workspace with the Single-Window Mode turned off, allowing the panels to be moved as needed.

Figure 3-5. *The GIMP workspace in the default Single-Window Mode*

Menus

The menus are located in the menu bar, which is found along the top of the workspace shown in Figure 3-6. Nearly every function available for GIMP can be accessed from one of the menus.

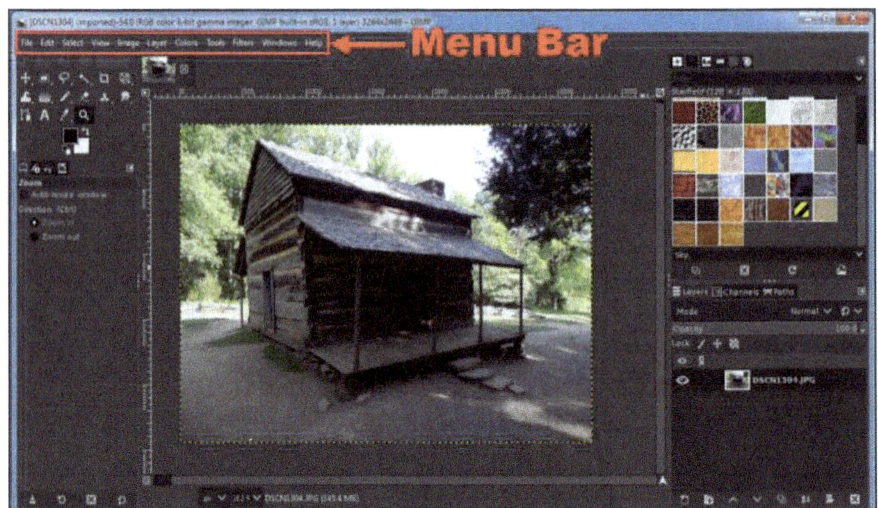

Figure 3-6. *The menus are located in the menu bar, which is found along the top of the workspace*

One example is the *Colors* menu, which contains a wide array of dialogs used for making tonal and color adjustments. Figure 3-7 shows an example of the *Shadows-Highlights* dialog being used to lighten the darkest areas of the image without affecting the other parts.

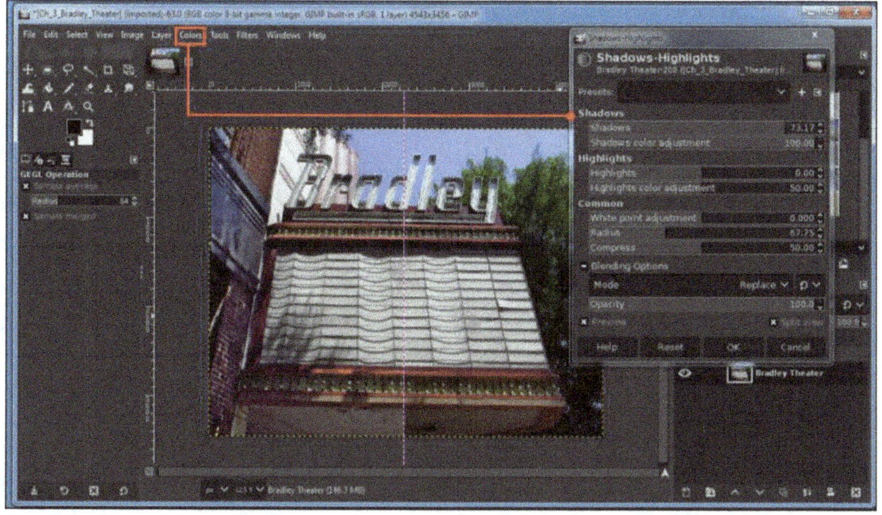

Figure 3-7. *The Shadows-Highlights dialog can be accessed from the Colors menu*

Another example is the *Filters* menu, which contains a wide array of *submenus*. These submenus contain dialogs used for applying special effects to the image. For instance, *Photocopy* is one of the *Artistic* filters used for applying artistic effects to the image (Figure 3-8).

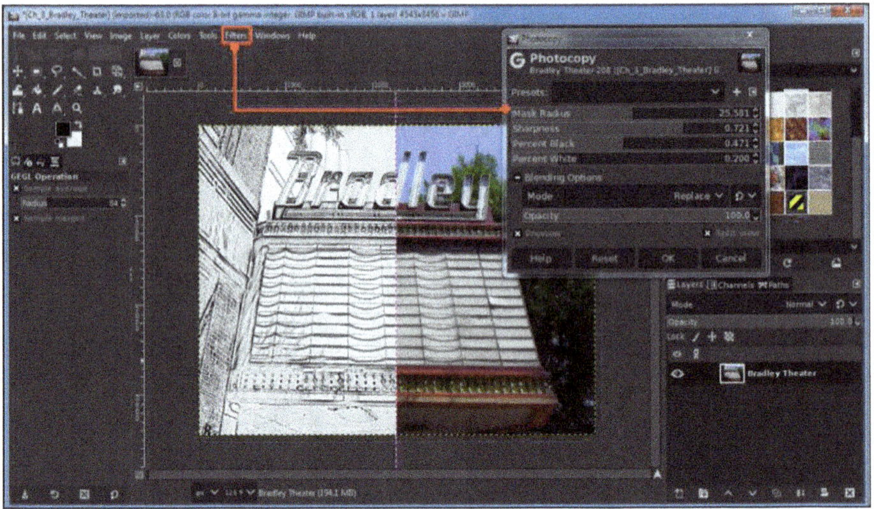

Figure 3-8. *Photocopy is one of the Artistic effects available under Filters*

Tools and Tool Settings

GIMP offers an impressive set of tools for precision image editing and creation. One example is the *Healing* tool, which is ideal for removing blemishes and other imperfections from portraits or casual photos. In Figure 3-9, the Healing tool is being used to remove the markings from the child's face.

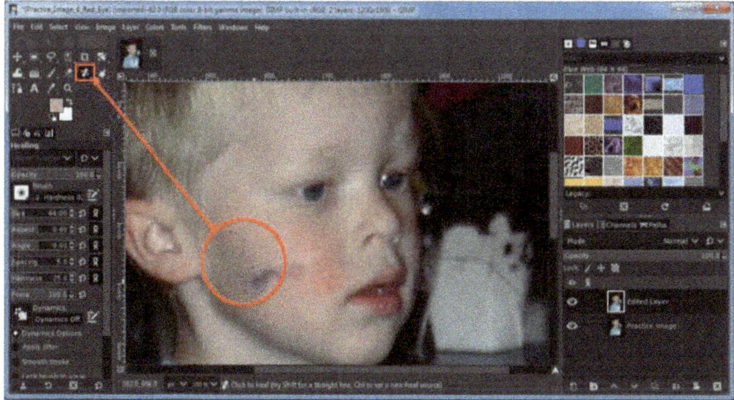

Figure 3-9. *The Healing tool is useful for removing blemishes and other imperfections. (Image courtesy of the Cash Family)*

As depicted in the before-and-after example, the Healing tool is well suited for portrait touch-up work (Figure 3-10).

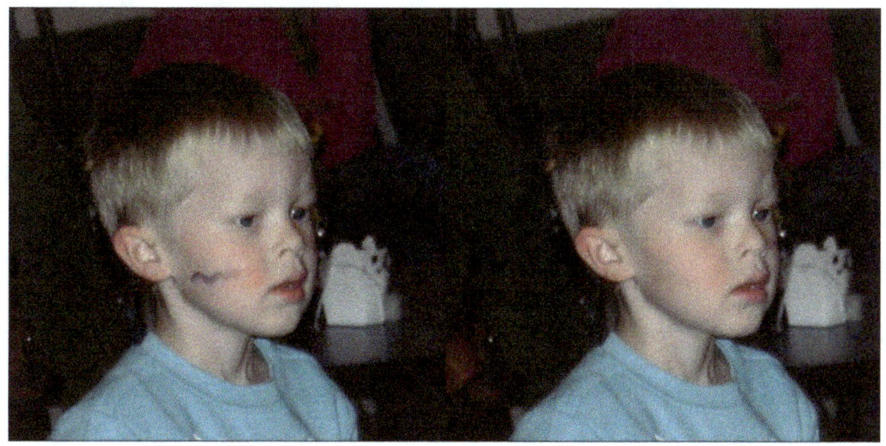

Figure 3-10. *Before-and-after comparison. (Image courtesy of the Cash Family)*

In GIMP, most of the tools are nested in *tool groups* of related tools. A tool group is indicated by a small triangle in the lower right corner. As shown in Figure 3-11, the *Clone* and *Perspective Clone* tools are in the same group as the Healing tool.

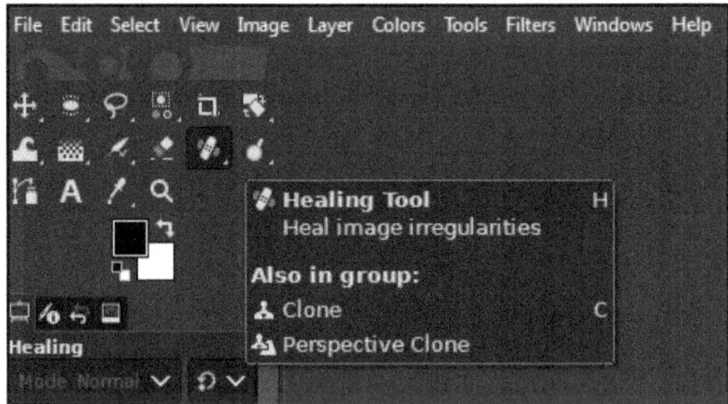

Figure 3-11. *Related tools are nested in tool groups*

Most of GIMP's tools have a corresponding dialog to adjust the parameters of the tool, affecting its behavior. Figure 3-12 displays the settings for the Healing tool, allowing the brush opacity, size, aspect ratio, and other parameters to be adjusted.

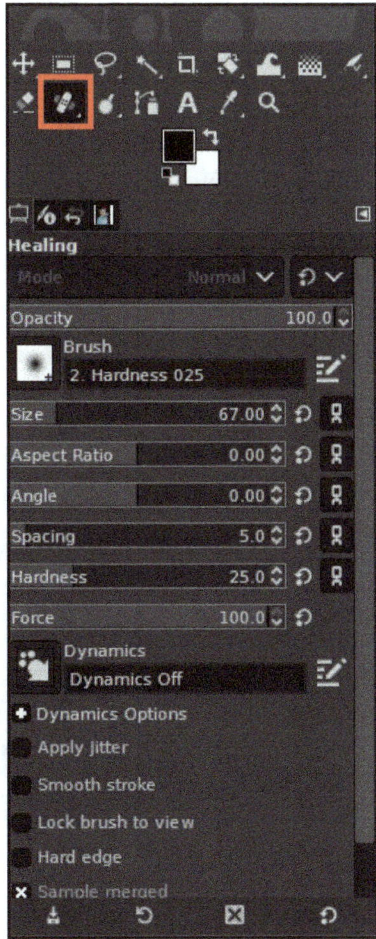

***Figure 3-12.** Most of GIMP's tools have a dialog to customize the settings, affecting the tool's behavior*

To learn more about the tools and how they function, in-depth information about GIMP's tools can be accessed here: `https://docs.gimp.org/2.10/en/gimp-tools.html#gimp-toolbox`.

Layers

GIMP offers a layer system, enabling users to create complex images. If you completed the tutorial in the previous chapter, you should be familiar with Paint.NET's layer system, which is similar to that of GIMP. However, GIMP's layer system is more advanced and offers additional features.

For example, GIMP provides a wide variety of layer *blend modes*, which influence how pixels interact with each other. Blend modes can be useful for creating interesting effects. Figure 3-13 demonstrates how placing an image of moviegoers over the marquee of a historic movie theater can result in an intriguing composite by changing the blend mode to hard light and lowering the opacity to about 81%.

Figure 3-13. *GIMP's layer blend modes can be used for creating intriguing effects*

In GIMP, complex images often consist of numerous layers, which can be effectively managed using GIMP's layer tools. One such tool is *layer groups*, which function like folders in the Layers palette, allowing related layers to be contained and organized within them.

Additionally, GIMP offers *color tags*, which provide a method of organizing and managing layers through a color-coded system. Color tags allow you to visually categorize layers based on their content or purpose.

By assigning color tags to layers, you can easily distinguish between different types of layers and quickly locate specific ones within your project. This can help streamline your workflow and work more efficiently on images with a large number of layers. Figure 3-14 shows several text layers color coded using color tags.

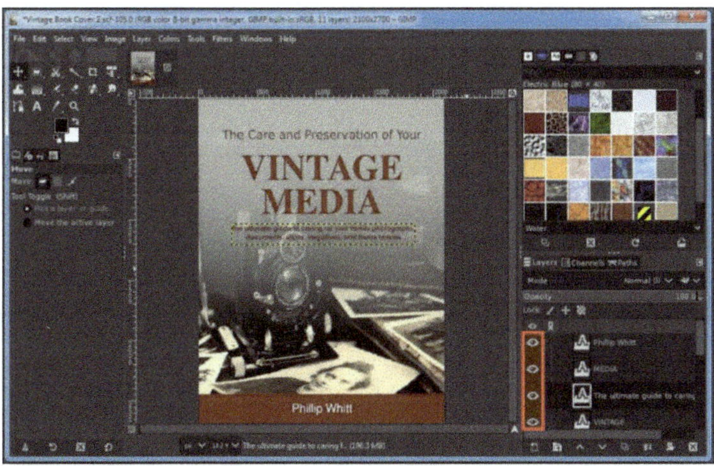

Figure 3-14. *Layer color tags help to manage and organize layers*

GIMP Tutorials

GIMP is a powerful, complex image editor that can be overwhelming to new users. Fortunately, there are numerous tutorials available that are worth taking the time to learn.

The best place to start is the official GIMP website, where several tutorials for beginners will help you navigate this powerful program. You can visit the page here: (`https://www.gimp.org/tutorials/`).

Another valuable source for tutorials is GIMP Guru. While many tutorials are for older versions of GIMP and primarily focused on photography, they are still applicable. You can access GIMP Guru's tutorials here: (`https://gimpguru.wordpress.com/tutorials/`).

Summary

Here's a brief recap of what was covered in this chapter:

- An introduction to GIMP (including the pros and cons)
- The GIMP workspace (which glanced at menus, tools, tool settings, and layers).
- GIMP tutorials

In the next chapter, we'll cover FotoSketcher, a free, easy-to-use program that turns photos into digital art.

CHAPTER 4

FotoSketcher: Turn Photos into Art

This chapter explores a free and fun Windows program called *FotoSketcher*, which is used to turn photos into digital paintings, sketches, and other types of digital art. Here's what we'll touch on in this chapter:

- An introduction to FotoSketcher
- The FotoSketcher workspace
    - Menus
    - Drawing parameters
    - Other FotoSketcher features
- FotoSketcher tutorials
- Summary

An Introduction to FotoSketcher

FotoSketcher is a free, Windows-based program that offers over 20 artistic effects that can be applied to digital photographs. This application should not be confused with *PhotoSketcher*, a similar program for use on iOS devices; PhotoSketcher is a paid application provided by a different developer.

P. Whitt, *Cost-Effective Graphic Solutions for Small Businesses*, Apress Pocket Guides,
https://doi.org/10.1007/979-8-8688-1192-0_4

FotoSketcher (created by David Thoiron) is an award-winning program that's free to use for both personal and commercial purposes. Figure 4-1 shows a side-by-side comparison of the original image and a digitally "painted" version; images can be saved in the JPEG, PNG, or bitmapped file formats.

***Figure 4-1.** A comparison of the original image and the digitally "painted" version*

Note Although FotoSketcher is designed for Windows, it can run on Linux systems using WINE, a compatibility layer for Windows applications. I have successfully used it on Zorin OS without encountering any issues. However, it's worth noting that FotoSketcher's performance may vary depending on the specific Linux distribution.

While both Paint.NET and GIMP offer several filters for adding artistic effects to photographic images, FotoSketcher provides even more options, allowing users not only to create stunning digital art but also to combine effects for unique creations. Figure 4-2 shows a comparison of the source image (left), the image with the *vintage photo* effect applied (center), and the result of merging the two (right).

Figure 4-2. *Comparison of the source image, the image with the vintage photo effect applied, and the merging of both versions*

FotoSketcher can be a useful companion application for other editing software programs. The output version of the image processed in FotoSketcher shown earlier was combined with a stock image of a wooden wall and further modified using GIMP to create a rustic-themed Facebook cover image of a fictitious farm growing organic products (Figure 4-3).

Figure 4-3. *The output version of the image was combined with an image of a wooden wall and modified in GIMP to create this rustic-themed graphic*

FotoSketcher is an impressive, easy-to-use program for applying artistic filters to photographic images, but it does have a few limitations worth noting—here's a list of pros and cons to consider:

Pros

- Free to download and use for personal or commercial purposes; can be installed on as many computers as needed.
- FotoSketcher has a very low learning curve, so anyone can start using it straight away.
- The software is freeware and can be distributed to friends or coworkers. Charging money for the software is prohibited, but charging for the media it's delivered on is permitted.
- Utilizes a clean, uncluttered workspace that's easy to navigate.
- Easy to learn and use.

Cons

- Only runs on Windows, with the exception that it should run on Linux systems using WINE (although performance may vary).
- The program's output quality may be marginal if a low-quality source image is used.
- Large images can take a long time to process.
- Offers only three file export formats.

To download FotoSketcher, simply visit the download page here: `https://fotosketcher.com/download-fotosketcher/`.

The FotoSketcher Workspace

After FotoSketcher has been downloaded and installed, you will be greeted with a simple, easy to navigate workspace upon launching. By default, the source image is displayed in the left panel and the result in the right panel (Figure 4-4).

Figure 4-4. *The FotoSketcher workspace is simple and easy to navigate*

The *Change window style* setting under the Edit menu allows you to change the theme from *Obsidian* (the default setting) to *Charcoal, Slate,* or *Light* (Figure 4-5).

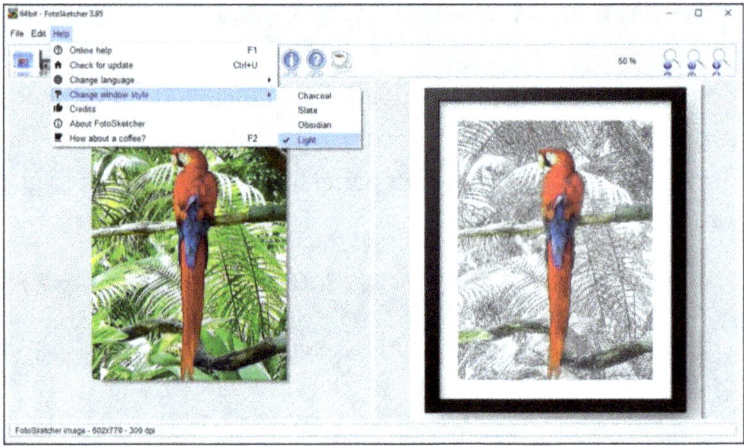

Figure 4-5. *The Window style can be customized from the default Obsidian theme to Charcoal, Slate, or Light*

Menus

FotoSketcher's menus (*File, Edit,* and *Help*) are located along the top area of the workspace as shown in Figure 4-6. All of the program's functions are found under the corresponding menu; for example, *Drawing parameters* submenu can be found under the Edit menu.

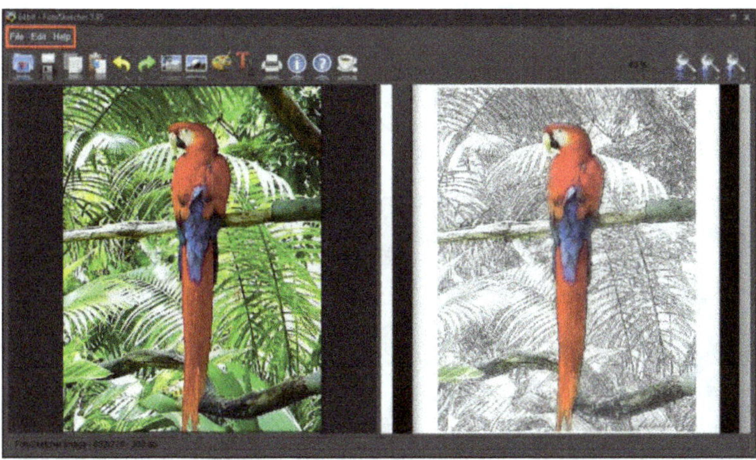

Figure 4-6. *The menus are located along the top of the workspace indicated*

Just below the menus (Figure 4-7), there is a bank of *icons* that contain commonly used functions (also housed in the menus), providing quick access to these features. On the right is a set of tools for zooming out, viewing at 1:1 ratio (100%), and zooming in.

Figure 4-7. *The icons indicated allow quick access to commonly used features*

It's beyond the scope of this chapter to cover all the functions, but there are a couple I'll touch on because they are useful for altering the source image before an effect is applied. One such feature is *Crop to selection*, which allows you to trim the image down as necessary (Figure 4-8).

Figure 4-8. *The Crop to selection feature allows you to trim the image as necessary*

Another such feature is *Modify source image*, which allows you to increase or decrease *Luminosity, Contrast, Saturation*, as well as adjust the *Blur/Sharpen* and *Simplification* (Figure 4-9).

Figure 4-9. *The Modify source image dialog allows you to make tonal adjustments, as well as blur, sharpen, and simplify the image*

Drawing Parameters

The *Drawing parameters* is where most of the "digital magic" takes place in FotoSketcher. Each effect falls under a category known as a *Drawing style,* in which there are several available: *Pencil sketch effects, Pen & Ink sketch effects, Painting effects, Stylized effects, Miscellaneous effects,* and *No effect (Frame, texture, and text only).*

Figure 4-10 depicts the *Drawing parameters* menu; placing the cursor over the effect displays a small preview window of the results.

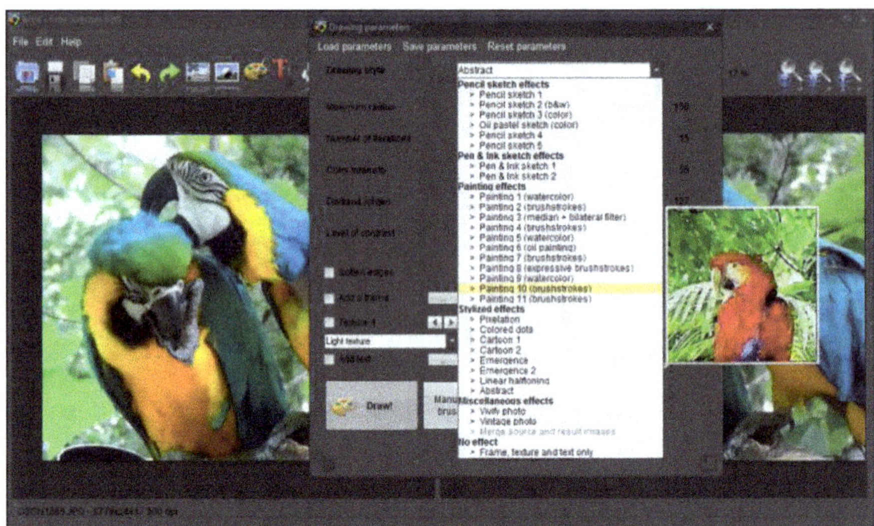

Figure 4-10. *The Drawing parameters menu; a small preview window of the effect is displayed when hovering the cursor over the effect title*

Each effect has a set of parameters that can be adjusted to achieve the result you'd like. The parameters vary from one effect to the next, but *Maximum brush size* and *Number of iterations* are common to most. Figure 4-11 shows the parameters of the *Painting 10 (brushstrokes)* effect.

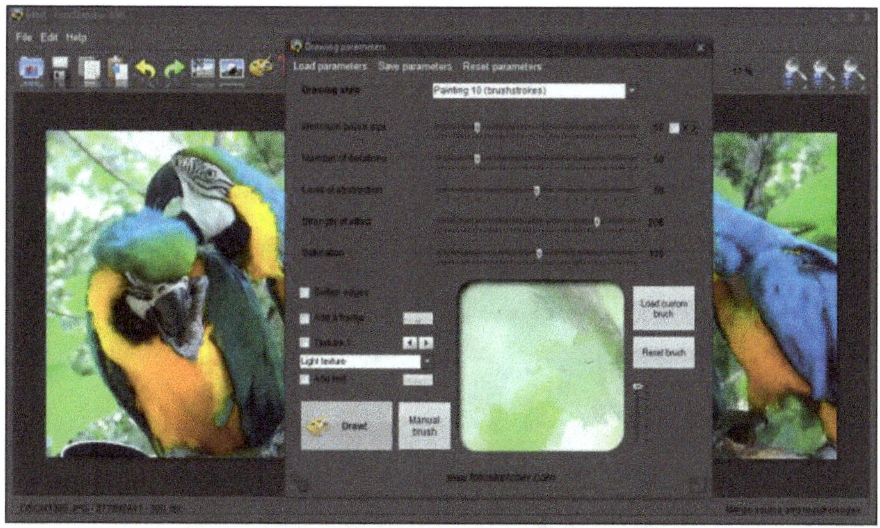

Figure 4-11. *The parameters of the Painting 10 (brushstrokes) effect*

Some experimentation with the settings may be necessary to achieve the desired outcome. In those instances, the parameters can be saved once the desired result is achieved and reused for other projects. FotoSketcher's parameters can also be reset to their default settings.

Other FotoSketcher Features

Also found in the Drawing parameters menu, there are several additional functions used to soften the image edges, adding frames, adding texture, and adding text. Here's a glance at each feature:

- *Soften edges* helps smooth out the edges in the digital artwork created in FotoSketcher, resulting in a more realistic appearance.

- *Add a frame* provides a selection of picture frame styles that can be added to your image. Some aspects can be customized, such as the color and size of the matte. Figure 4-12 provides an example of a realistic frame added to the image.

Figure 4-12. *An example of a realistic frame added to the image*

- *Texture* provides an assortment of realistic textures that can be added to your image and can be set to *light, normal,* or *strong*. Figure 4-13 shows an example of a texture set to strong applied to the digital painting of the old farm cart shown earlier in this chapter.

Figure 4-13. *An example of a digital painting before and then after a texture is applied*

- *Text* allows the user to apply text over the processed images if desired. The user can choose the font (typeface), size, and color. Figure 4-14 shows an example of text being added to the image.

Figure 4-14. *An example of adding text to an image*

FotoSketcher Tutorials

FotoSketcher is a relatively easy program to learn, but new users may benefit from some guidance. The ideal place to familiarize yourself with this program is the website; to view what's possible with this program, visit the *Gallery* page here: `https://fotosketcher.com/fotosketcher-gallery/`.

There are several video tutorials that can be viewed on the *Help* page here: `https://fotosketcher.com/fotosketcher-help/`.

If you'd like to learn FotoSketcher in greater depth, you might be interested in my video course, *Digital Art Creation Using FotoSketcher*, available through the Apress subscription program. For more information, visit: `https://link.springer.com/video/10.1007/978-1-4842-8284-7`.

Summary

Here's a brief recap of what was covered in this chapter:

- An introduction to FotoSketcher (including the pros and cons)
- The FotoSketcher workspace (which glanced at menus, drawing parameters, and other FotoSketcher features)
- FotoSketcher tutorials

In the next chapter, we'll cover Inkscape, a free vector illustration program.

CHAPTER 5

Inkscape: The Free Program for Creating Scalable Vector Graphics

This chapter explores the free and open source program Inkscape, which is a free alternative to Adobe Illustrator. Unlike Paint.NET and GIMP which work with *raster* images (such as photographs), Inkscape is designed for vector drawing. Here's what we'll cover in this chapter:

- An introduction to Inkscape
- An introduction to vector graphics
- The Inkscape workspace
    - Menus
    - Tools and tool settings
- Inkscape tutorials
- Summary

P. Whitt, *Cost-Effective Graphic Solutions for Small Businesses*, Apress Pocket Guides,
https://doi.org/10.1007/979-8-8688-1192-0_5

An Introduction to Inkscape

Adobe Illustrator is the premier tool for creating vector graphics among professional designers. Of course, it does come with a subscription cost, which starts at about $22.99 per month. It's reasonable to presume many small business owners wouldn't require access to this program on a regular basis, which would make it an unnecessary ongoing expense. Inkscape is a free, open source alternative for creating scalable vector graphics. Figure 5-1 shows an example of an illustration created using Inkscape.

Figure 5-1. *An example of an illustration created in Inkscape*

Like GIMP, Inkscape is a free, open source program that can be installed on an unlimited number of computers and enjoy the same General Public License benefits as those offered with GIMP.

Inkscape is a popular program used by freelance professionals, hobbyists, and business owners. It's a powerful program, but it is rather complex as well. Here are the pros and cons to Inkscape:

Pros

- Free to download and use for personal or commercial purposes; can be installed on as many computers as needed
- Can be freely copied and distributed according to the terms of the General Public License (GPL)
- A powerful vector drawing program that can serve as a viable alternative to Adobe Illustrator in many cases
- Advanced features capable of producing professional results
- Can be installed on Windows, macOS, and Linux

Cons

- Steep learning curve can make it difficult for new users to learn.
- Large, complex drawings can bog down computer resources.
- Inkscape updates may be somewhat irregular; in their defense, Inkscape is developed and maintained by volunteers with regular jobs, so they must update the program as time allows.

To download Inkscape, simply visit the website here: `https://inkscape.org/`.

An Introduction to Vector Graphics

Inkscape is a professional grade illustration program used for creating *scalable vector graphics*, which means they can be scaled up or down without loss of quality (Figure 5-2). These types of graphics are based on mathematical formulas, so a graphic that starts out small can be enlarged as much as you'd like. However, raster graphics lose detail if they are scaled up or down too much.

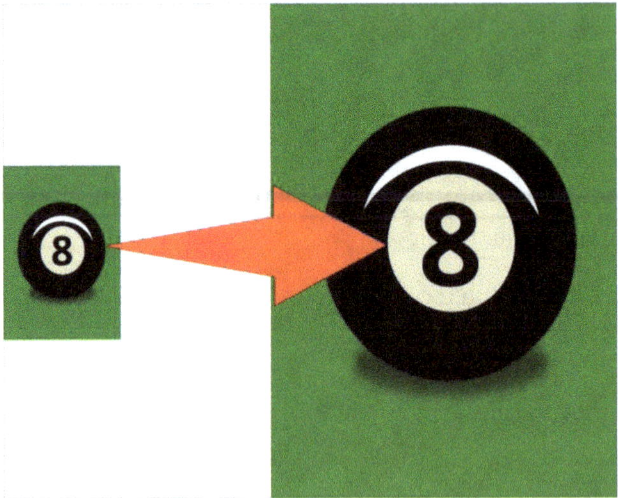

***Figure 5-2.** Scalable vector graphics can be scaled up or down without loss of image quality*

When raster images are enlarged (or scaled down), they can show noticeably jagged edges. Figure 5-3 shows a comparison of an enlarged area of the billiard ball illustration—the example on the left is a vector file, and the version on the right a raster version, which clearly has jagged edges.

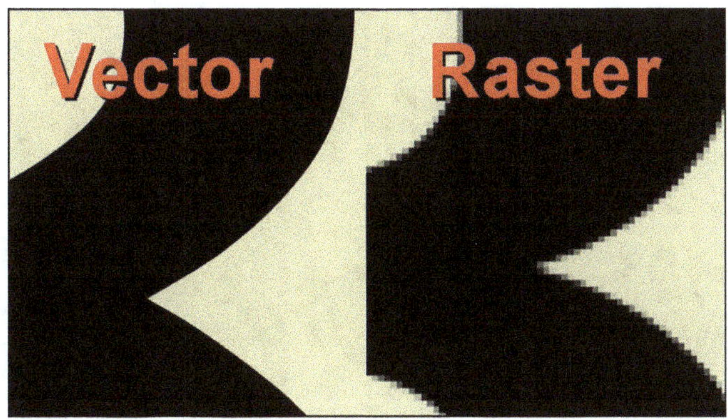

Figure 5-3. *Comparison of a magnified view of a vector image and a raster image*

The Inkscape Workspace

Inkscape is a full-featured program, so new users may find the workspace a bit overwhelming. If you have experience using Adobe Illustrator or Corel Draw, then learning Inkscape shouldn't be too difficult.

Like most modern drawing programs, Inkscape uses a dark-themed workspace (Figure 5-4), which helps reduce eyestrain, improve focus on the artwork, and can help improve color perception.

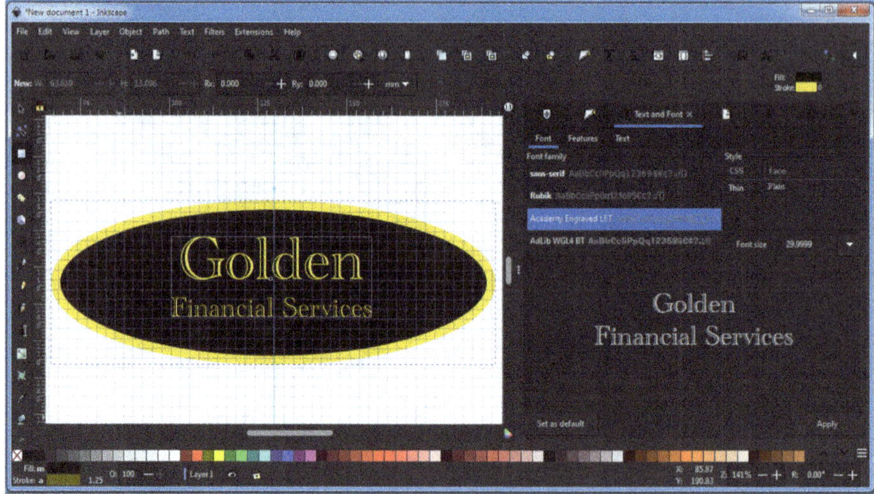

Figure 5-4. *Inkscape uses a dark-themed workspace*

Figure 5-5 indicates where most of Inkscape's main areas are in the workspace:

- The application *menu bar* is located along the top and provides general menu options such as *File, Edit, View,* etc. It also contains features specific to Inkscape.
- The *rulers* are placed along the top and on the left of the canvas, to help with grid and guideline placement.
- The *toolbox* is a vertical panel on the left side of the workspace. It contains the main drawing and creating shapes.
- The *page area* is represented by a white triangle.
- The large blank area (containing the page area) is the *canvas,* where image editing takes place.
- The *palette* is located near the bottom of the window; it's used to change the fill color of an object.

- The *status bar* is located at the very bottom and displays information such as the colors of the selected object, layers, cursor coordinates, zoom level, and page rotation. It also provides information such as the number and type of selected objects and tips on using a selected tool, as well as its keyboard shortcut.

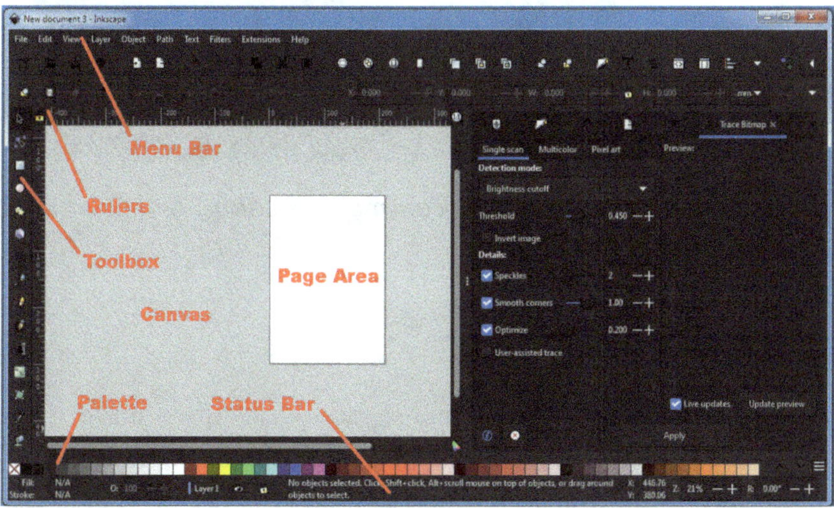

***Figure 5-5.** This figure indicates the location of most Inkscape's main areas*

Menus

The menus are accessed from the menu bar along the top of the workspace. In addition to common functions such as opening and saving files, copying, and pasting, there are functions such as working with objects and paths, editing text, and applying *filters* (adding special effects to the object). Figure 5-6 shows an example of various filters applied to a group of circles to create the appearance of different materials.

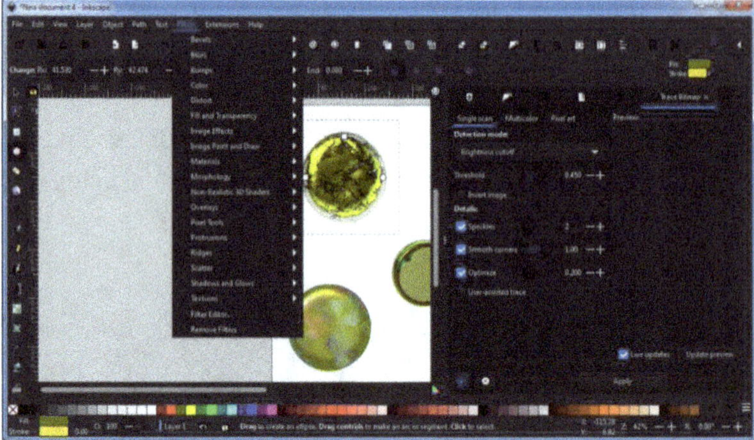

Figure 5-6. *The menus contain common functions, as well as filters used for applying special effects*

Tools and Tool Settings

The tools are accessed from the toolbox, located on the left side of the window. There are tools for creating shapes, curves, freehand drawing, text, and more. When a specific tool is active, the *tool settings* bar displays the corresponding settings. Figure 5-7 shows the tool used for creating stars and polygons and the settings to adjust the number of corners, rounding the corners, and randomizing the corners and angles.

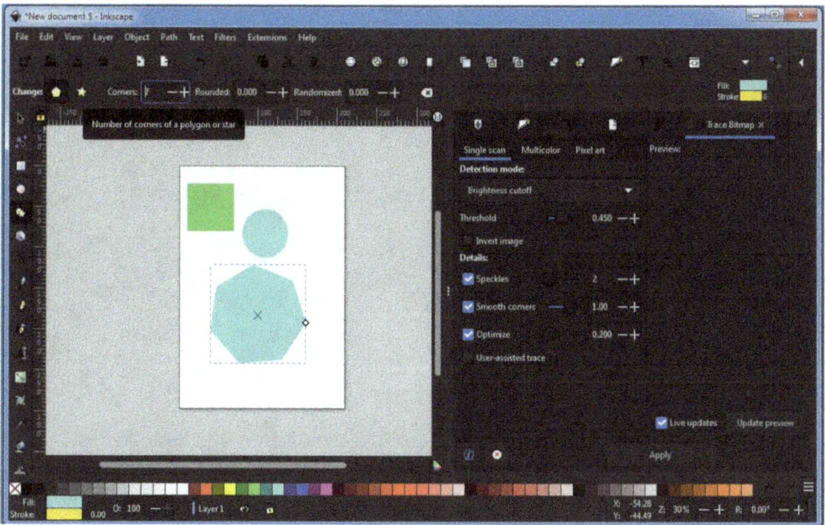

Figure 5-7. *When a specific tool is active, the setting can be adjusted using the tool settings bar*

Inkscape Tutorials

For new users, the best place to start becoming acquainted with Inkscape is to access the tutorials from the menu. Simply click *Help*, and navigate to the *Tutorials* submenu. When it launches, you'll see a number of tutorials, starting with *Basic* (Figure 5-8).

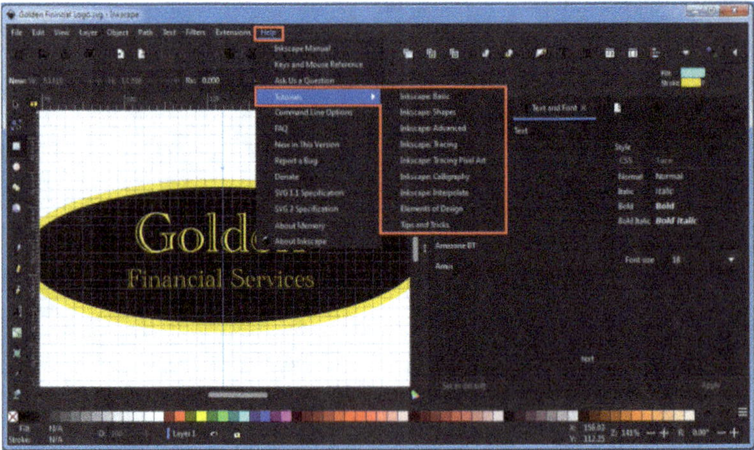

Figure 5-8. *Inkscape tutorials can be found under the Help menu*

Another valuable learning resource is *The Inkscape Beginner's Guide*, which can be found here: `https://inkscape-manuals.readthedocs.io/en/latest/`.

Summary

In this chapter, we took a brief tour of Inkscape, a popular free alternative to Adobe Illustrator. Here's what we covered:

- An introduction to Inkscape (including the pros and cons)
- An introduction to vector graphics
- The Inkscape workspace
    - Menus
    - Tools and tool settings
- Inkscape tutorials

In the next chapter, we'll cover several affordable web-based solutions for creating effective (and low-cost) designs.

PART III

Using Predesigned Templates, Stock Images and AI, and Resources for Large Format Graphics

CHAPTER 6

Affordable Web-Based Solutions

In recent years, web-based graphic creation programs have gained in popularity. Because they operate within your computer's browser, it's not necessary to install a separate program, and they are compatible across all operating systems, making them convenient to access.

In this chapter, you'll be introduced to three web-based design solutions that are extremely useful and budget-friendly. Here are the topics we'll explore:

- A brief introduction to Canva
  - A few of Canva's features
  - Utilizing AI applications in Canva
- A brief introduction to Pixlr
  - A glance at some of Pixlr's features
  - A brief look at Pixlr's AI image generator
- A brief introduction to Marq (formerly Lucidpress)
  - A glance at Marq's templates
  - Marq's pricing plans
- Summary

P. Whitt, *Cost-Effective Graphic Solutions for Small Businesses*, Apress Pocket Guides,
https://doi.org/10.1007/979-8-8688-1192-0_6

A Brief Introduction to Canva

Canva is a web-based design tool used for creating posters, flyers, business cards, social media posts, as well as other personal, marketing, and business communication materials. There was a time that graphic design required a professional designer or firm to create these kinds of materials. Fortunately, Canva was designed with small business owners in mind, particularly those lacking graphic design expertise. Canva empowers them to produce high-quality designs independently—no expensive graphic design firm needed. Explore Canva's home page for more information: `https://www.canva.com/`.

A Few of Canva's Features

Canva offers a wide variety of predesigned templates—the user can then drag and drop images in place, as well as edit and format the text.

Many of the features offered in Canva are free to use, allowing the user to try it out and familiarize themselves with the platform. Canva Pro requires a paid subscription to unlock the premium features, which are indicated by a small crown-shaped icon.

Canva offers just about everything you need to create professional quality marketing materials and presentations. Figure 6-3 showcases several Instagram video reel templates.

Here's a partial list of what Canva can help you create:

- Business cards
- Flyers
- Posters
- Social media posts
- Infographics
- Brand templates
- Website creation

Canva offers a variety of templates for business communications such as annual reports, employee booster kits, finance fulfillment, invoices, and more

Utilizing AI Applications in Canva

Canva integrates with numerous applications that allow the user to harness the power of AI in the creation of their marketing and promotional materials—everything from image creation to realistic "talking head" videos that can be incorporated into your designs.

One notable example is that Canva now integrates with DALL-E, an advanced AI image generation tool created by OpenAI. DALL-E can generate incredibly lifelike images, offering two versions based on the descriptions provided in the prompt field.

Canva integrates with a wide variety of AI applications designed to enhance your presentations and make your work easier.

Here's a partial list of several other AI applications that Canva integrates with:

- D-ID AI Presenters (AI-generated avatars)
- Imagen (AI image generator by Google)
- Magic Media (AI media generator)
- Avatars by NeirdoAI (generates video avatars to represent your speech)
- Magic Morph (AI style generator)
- Mojo AI (AI and QR art generator)
- Murf AI (Text to speech voice generator)
- Soundraw (AI music generator)

There are numerous other AI applications available to bolster your Canva creations. Discover the full range of possibilities here: `https://www.canva.com/your-apps/ai-powered`.

Note Before utilizing any AI apps for commercial use, I strongly urge reviewing their Terms of Service beforehand. This is crucial because some companies might claim ownership to the final output, making it imperative to conduct proper due diligence beforehand.

Canva offers a range of pricing plans scaled to different needs. Among these, the most popular option is Canva Pro, currently priced at $14.99 per month for individual use; purchasing annually at $119.99 saves 16%.

A Brief Introduction to Pixlr

Similar to Canva in many respects, Pixlr is a suite of web-based tools that are used for image editing, creation, and template-based design. Pixlr also offers a number of AI tools, one of which is an image generator capable of outputting highly realistic results.

Pixlr Editor was originally founded in 2008 as a browser-based photo editing program similar to Adobe Photoshop. Since that time, Pixlr has expanded into a family of products that not only include the flagship online photo editor but tools such as *Pixlr Express, Pixlr Designer, Remove Background,* and *Batch Editor*.

Many of Pixlr's features are available for free, but a paid subscription is required to access the premium features. To explore Pixlr in more depth, visit the home page here: `https://pixlr.com/`.

A Glance at Some of Pixlr's Features

Pixlr Editor is an advanced photo editing tool similar to Adobe Photoshop. It boasts a number of tools and features useful for detailed image editing work, including the *Heal* tool, which is highly effective for portrait retouching and removing unwanted objects, such as the fence depicted in Figure 6-1.

***Figure 6-1.** The Heal tool is very useful for portrait retouching and removing unwanted objects*

While Pixlr Editor is best suited for those with image editing experience, *Pixlr Express* is a slimmed-down image editing tool aimed more at casual and novice users. It offers a sleek set of basic editing tools, but where it really shines is in its set of AI tools, designed to make editing work go much faster and easier.

Here's a list of the AI tools available to help enhance the image editing experience using Pixlr Express:

- Generative fill (select an area and enter a prompt to fill the area with an image of your description; results can be unpredictable).

- Generative expand (expand the image in any direction; Pixlr's AI will fill in the void).
- Face swap/AI avatar (switches faces from one person to another).
- Generative transform (separate an object from the image and move, resize, or rotate them freely).
- Backdrop (add a blur, motion, depth, or generate a new background).
- Remove object (draw a selection around an object and is seamlessly removed).
- Super scale (uses AI to upscale images and retain high quality).
- Super sharp (improves images that are slightly out of focus).
- Remove noise (automatically removes grain and reduces background noise from images).

Figure 6-2 shows a comparison of the original image and then the same image widened using the *Generative Expand* feature. Images can be expanded in any direction.

Figure 6-2. *The Generative Expand feature utilizes AI to widen the image*

Pixlr's AI tools cost credits to use (usually one, two, or four, depending on the tool being utilized). With the Premium paid subscription, 1000 AI credits are issued each month.

Pixlr Designer offers several features that small business owners can easily utilize and appreciate: *Photo Collage Maker, Product Shot, Templates, Open file,* and *Start New.*

Figure 6-3 depicts an example of a design utilizing an AI-generated image and the Text Tool in Pixlr Designer.

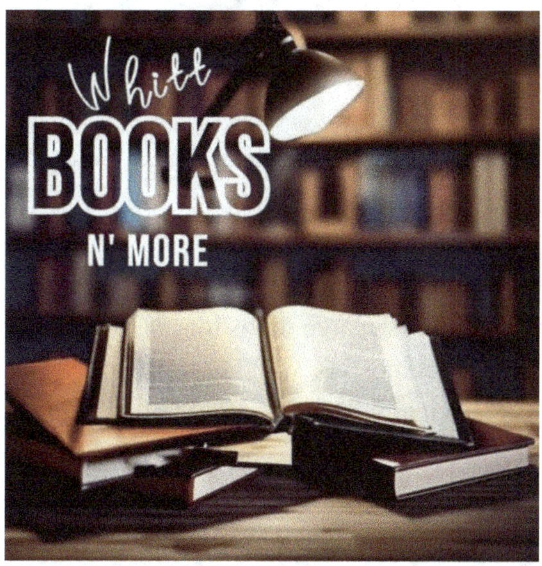

Figure 6-3. *This design utilizes an AI-generated image and the Text tool in Pixlr Designer*

One especially useful feature for anyone who sells physical items is Product Shot, which allows you to digitally place an image on a professional-looking background (Figure 6-4). The background can be selected from the library, or a new AI-generated background can be output.

Figure 6-4. *Product Shot is a useful feature for business owners that sell physical items*

Pixlr Designer contains a large repository of predesigned templates social media posts, flyers, posters, vouchers, and much more. There's a template for just about anything one would need, for personal or business use.

A Brief Look at Pixlr's AI Image Generator

The AI image generator is capable of creating impressive output and is an effective tool that can enhance the visual communications employed by small business owners.

There are numerous options available, such as *Aspect*, *Style*, *Color*, *Lighting*, and *Composition*. There's an option to load an existing image (this influences the results of the output of the generated images) and an option for *Random prompt*, *Negative prompt* (this allows you to input what you don't want in the final output), and *Make private*—output images are made public by default.

Each prompt costs four credits and will generate four versions of the image. Figure 6-5 displays four versions of an image based on the prompt "Hanging potted ferns."

Figure 6-5. *Four versions of an image generated using Pixlr 's AI Image Generator*

The AI Image Generator is a useful feature that integrates nicely into the Pixlr suite. This can be useful for generating images when a suitable stock photo isn't available.

By using Pixlr Editor to modify one of the output images, Pixlr Designer was then used to create this example of how a small hardware store or nursery can utilize this suite to create eye-catching signage (Figure 6-6).

Figure 6-6. *An example of how an AI-generated image could be used in eye-catching retail signage*

Pixlr offers several subscription plans, the most popular being the Premium Plan for a single user at $7.99 per month; when billed annually, you can save 38%, which translates to $4.90 per month.

Note We'll briefly touch on two other AI image generators in Chapter 8.

A Brief Introduction Marq (Formerly Lucidpress)

Marq is yet another design option for the budget-minded small business owner to consider. While it shares some similarities to Canva and Pixlr, Marq places more emphasis on branding, simplicity of use, and collaborating with team members.

Although Marq doesn't offer AI-driven tools or image editing capabilities like Canva and Pixlr, there are plenty of robust features. Business owners or managers can create postcards, flyers, business cards, and other types of marketing and visual communications.

You can also manage your projects, images, brand assets, and perform analytics on how your organization uses content. *Marq for Team* offers data automation, eliminating the need to manually enter information, and helps streamline document creation. To learn more about Marq, visit the home page: `https://www.marq.com`.

After landing on the home page, you can sign up for a free account to begin using some of the limited features to try it out (Figure 6-7).

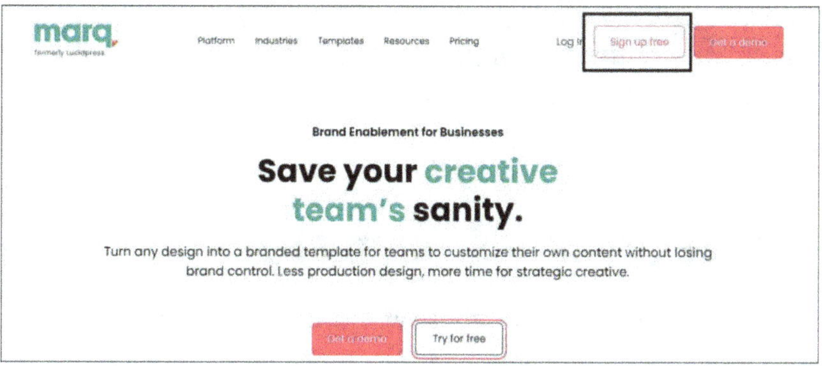

Figure 6-7. *After landing on Marq's home page, simply sign up for a free account to try it out. (Image courtesy of Marq)*

After creating your account, a window launches (Figure 6-8) allowing you to start creating your content by assessing one of the many templates available (some features are available only on a paid plan). There are also tutorials available to help you market your business better, as well as access the *Video Library* to help develop greater proficiency using this platform.

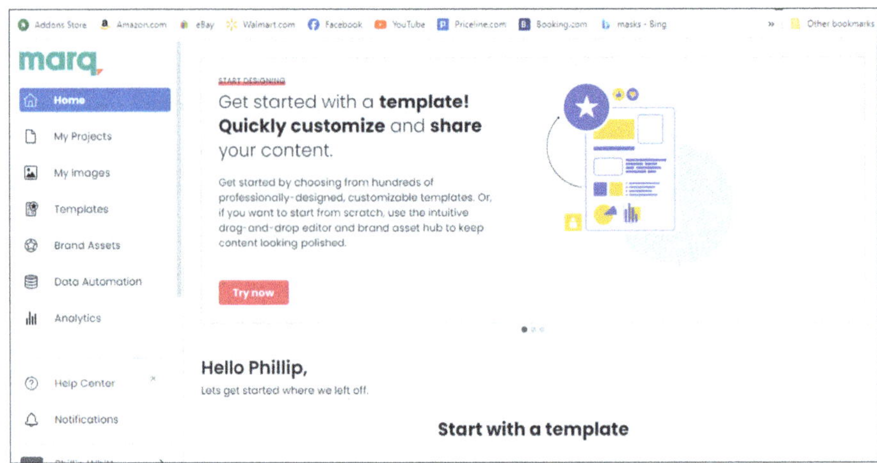

Figure 6-8. *After creating an account, this window launches, allowing you to start creating content by accessing the Templates library. (Image courtesy of Marq)*

A Glance at Marq's Templates

Marq is an excellent option for those with little experience in graphic by offering a wide range of predesigned templates. Simply choose a template based on industry, and you can customize the content to suit your business. Figure 6-9 depicts an example of a predesigned flyer for child care services.

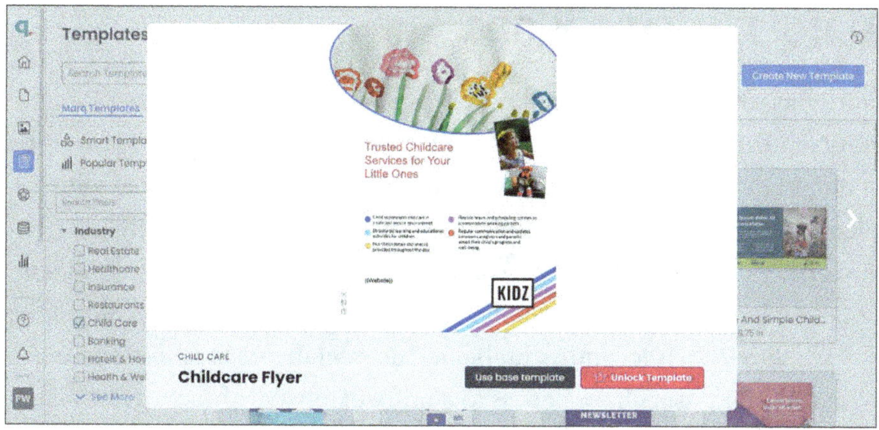

***Figure 6-9.** An example of a predesigned template for child care services. (Image courtesy of Marq)*

The template can customized by using your own images, editing text, and using your own logo.

Marq is also useful for those with design experience; you can create a new template from scratch or import from Adobe InDesign (Figure 6-10).

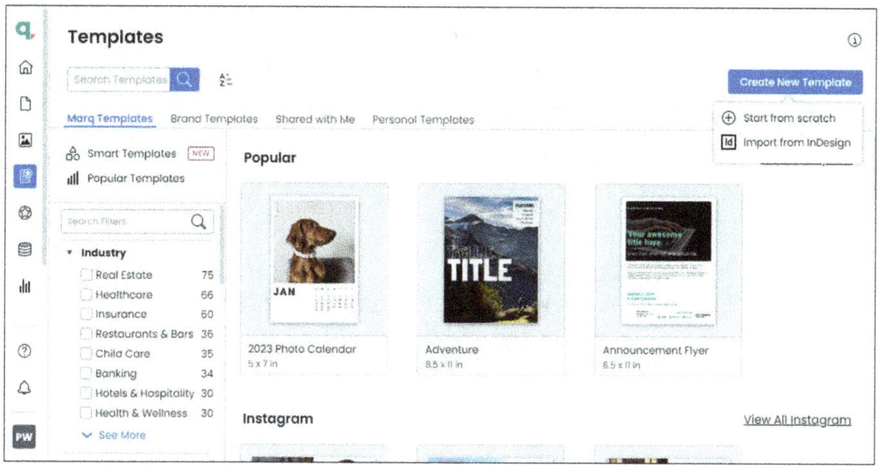

***Figure 6-10.** Those with more design experience can start a new template from scratch or import from Adobe InDesign. (Image courtesy of Marq)*

Marq's Pricing Plans

Marq has several pricing plans to suit a range of needs. The free plan grants individuals limited access to Marq's features and limits the number of document creation and storage to three. A free seven-day trial allows access to Marq's pro features for those considering a subscription. *At the time of this writing, Marq is conducting an A/B experiment with their pricing structure. The prices shown in this publication are subject to change.*

The *Pro Plan* is for individuals such as freelancers or solopreneurs. With this plan, users have access to a more extensive library of templates, fonts, and image editing capabilities. The plan is $10 per month when billed annually or $13 when billed monthly.

The *Team Plan* is for small organizations with up to ten team members. It includes all of the features of the Pro Plan, plus administrative and collaborative features to manage team projects. The Team Plan is $40 per month (billed annually) and $50 when billed monthly.

The *Business Plan* is designed for larger enterprises. It offers the same features as the Team Plan, plus more advanced collaboration features, as well as integration with third-party platforms such as Salesforce, Google Drive, and HubSpot. To learn more about pricing for the Business Plan, contact Marq's Sales Department.

Summary

Here's a brief recap of what was covered in this chapter:

- A brief introduction to Canva
- A brief introduction to Pixlr
- A brief introduction to Marq

In the next chapter, we'll explore several no-cost options for stock images you can unitize for your visual designs.

CHAPTER 7

No-Cost Stock Image Resources

Stock images are often necessary elements for designing marketing materials, but they can be a bit expensive for a small business operating on a shoestring budget. This chapter provides a brief overview of several sources to obtain no-cost stock illustrations and photographic images to incorporate into your designs. Here's a list of several popular sources we'll cover in this chapter:

- OpenClipArt
- Pexels
  - The Pexels license
- Pixabay
  - The Pixabay license
- Unsplash
  - The Unsplash license
- Summary

P. Whitt, *Cost-Effective Graphic Solutions for Small Businesses*, Apress Pocket Guides,
https://doi.org/10.1007/979-8-8688-1192-0_7

OpenClipArt

This site serves as an online repository of graphic illustrations available for both personal and commercial use at no cost. Established in 2004, the library is maintained by volunteers and now boasts over 160,000 images—to access the site, visit: `https://openclipart.org/`.

The images are typically available for download in two formats: SVG (Scalable Vector Graphics) files or PNG bitmapped images (which have a transparent background). The bicycle graphic (Figure 7-1) utilized in Chapter 2's exercise was sourced from this platform.

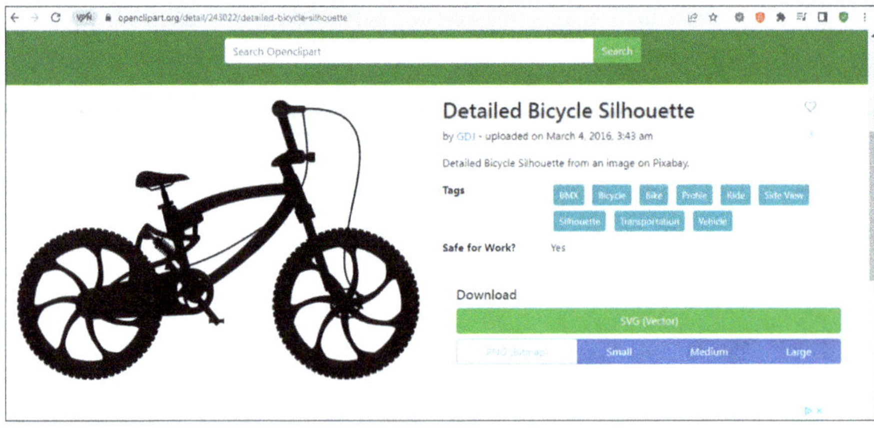

Figure 7-1. *The bicycle graphic used in Chapter 2's exercise was sourced from OpenClipArt*

The images contributed to this online resource are released into the public domain and fall under the Creative Commons license. This essentially means they can be used for any purpose—this includes unlimited commercial use. For more information, simply visit the FAQ page found here: `https://openclipart.org/share`.

Pexels

Pexels is a valuable resource for the budget-minded business by providing stock images and videos for both personal and commercial use at no cost (Figure 7-2). Although attribution to the contributor is generally not required, it is appreciated. Pexels was founded in 2014 and acquired by Canva in 2019. Currently, there are over three million photographic images and videos in the Pexels library which can be accessed here: `https://www.pexels.com/`.

Figure 7-2. *Photos and videos in the Pexels library are available to use for personal or commercial purposes at no cost—attribution to the contributor isn't required but is appreciated. (Screenshot courtesy of Pexels)*

When downloading an image, it can be imported directly into Canva for editing (a paid subscription is required to access the premium features) or simply downloaded to your computer or device. Figure 7-3 shows an example of a photographic image sourced from Pexels and incorporated into the design mock-up shown.

Figure 7-3. *An example of an image sourced from Pexels and incorporated into this design mock-up. (Photo contributed by Tim Douglas)*

The Pexels License

As mentioned earlier, the Pexels License allows the use of images for personal and commercial purposes at no cost, with no attribution to the contributor required. There are, however, some limitations to the use of images sourced from Pexels—one example is that you are not allowed to sell or distribute the images on a stand-alone basis without significant modification.

The Pexels License (and I strongly encourage reading it) can be found here: `https://www.pexels.com/license/`.

Pixabay

Similar to Pexels, Pixabay is another provider of over 4.4 million no-cost stock images and video, but it also provides sound effects, music files, and GIFs. Like Pexels, the content sourced from Pixabay may be used for personal or commercial purposes with no attribution to the contributor required. You can explore the Pixabay website here: `https://pixabay.com/`.

Like Pexels, the image can be imported into Canva or downloaded directly. Figure 7-4 shows several image previews on the Pixabay site.

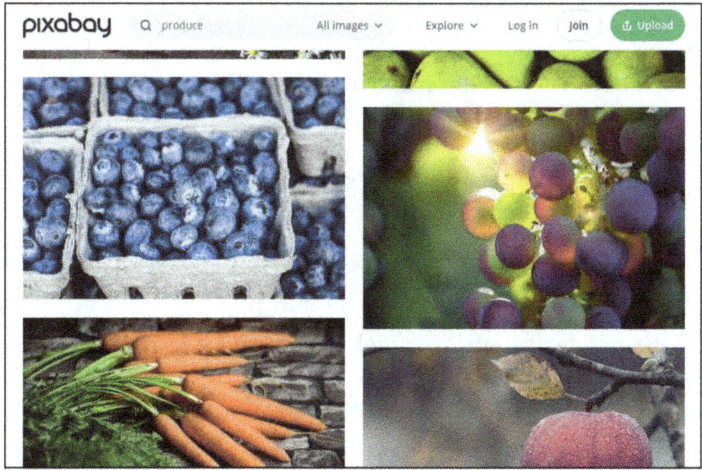

Figure 7-4. *Several image previews on the Pixabay site. (Screenshot courtesy of Pixabay)*

The Pixabay License

The terms under Pixabay's license are similar to those under the Pexels license. One stipulation worth noting under the Pixabay license is that it prohibits of using content in defamatory or unlawful ways or in a manner that suggests endorsement or affiliation with any products, brands, or entities.

The Pixabay License can be found here: `https://pixabay.com/service/license-summary/`.

Unsplash

Unsplash is yet another source of high-quality images, offering a more artistic and creative selection. It serves as a great resource for architectural and interior images, street photography, film photography, textures, patterns, and more.

This provider offers a paid subscription-based option called Unsplash+ (currently $7 per month) that offers additional benefits such as:

- New content added monthly for members only
- Unlimited downloads of royalty-free content
- Enhanced legal protections

Figure 7-5 shows an example of a stylized image contributed by Possessed Photography that was sourced from Unsplash and utilized in a concept business card. The Unsplash site can be explored here: `https://unsplash.com/`.

Figure 7-5. *This image was sourced from Unsplash and utilized for this concept business card*

The Unsplash License

The Unsplash license is similar (almost identical, actually) to those of Pexels and Pixabay—the license can be accessed here: `https://unsplash.com/license`.

Summary

We discovered the value of high-quality stock images available at no cost, offering a practical solution for small businesses to help reduce strain on the budget.

First, we looked at OpenClipArt, a source of illustrations available as SVG (Scalable Vector Graphics) and PNG files. Next, we looked at three sources of stock photographic images (as well as other resources, such as video, music, etc.) and the corresponding license agreements: Pexels, Pixabay, and Unsplash.

In the next chapter, we'll explore several real-world examples of work created by small companies using free and low-cost resources.

CHAPTER 8

Utilizing Generative AI Resources

This chapter touches on several resources for generating content using AI and how it can help you brainstorm ideas and create written content, images, and video for your visual communications.

Here's what we'll touch on in this chapter:

- A brief introduction to generative AI
- A brief introduction to ChatGPT
  - Effective prompt design
  - Brainstorming using ChatGPT
  - Generate the framework for written content using ChatGPT
  - Critique and evaluate designs using ChatGPT
- AI image and video generators
  - DALL-E 3
  - Generating content with Runway
- Ethical considerations
- Summary

P. Whitt, *Cost-Effective Graphic Solutions for Small Businesses*, Apress Pocket Guides,
https://doi.org/10.1007/979-8-8688-1192-0_8

A Brief Introduction to Generative AI

You have undoubtedly heard of AI (artificial intelligence), which has been at the cutting edge of computing technology in recent years, rapidly transforming entire industries. The recent advances in AI have resulted in a huge paradigm shift. While many people have a fundamental understanding of what AI is, a significant portion of the population only has a vague grasp of AI and its capabilities.

In this chapter, we'll focus on several resources for *generative AI*. Basically, generative AI is a subset of artificial intelligence used to create new content, such as generating text, images, video, and more based on a *prompt* provided to the AI system. A prompt is a text-based description of the content you want the AI to produce.

AI has actually been researched and developed since the 1950s, but it's only been in recent years that it has reached mainstream use thanks to advancements in computational power. Although not perfect, it continues to improve as time goes on. The underlying model for ChatGPT (GPT stands for generative pretrained transformer), developed by OpenAI, was released in 2020. Other similar AI systems (called chatbots) include *Perplexity* (not as well known but gaining in popularity), *Bing Chat*, and *Google Bard*.

Generative AI systems produce humanlike responses based on input *prompts*. A question, request, or description is typed into a field, and the AI system draws upon the vast data it has been trained on from the web, in books, and other sources to generate content that simulates conversing with a human. ChatGPT can be particularly useful for tasks such as creating the framework for sales copy, company policies, training guides, and more.

Image generators such as *DALL-E* (also developed by OpenAI), *Pixlr AI Image Generator* (which we touched on in Chapter 6), and *Runway* create prompt-based images. Utilizing generative AI can help small business owners create professional quality visual communications that are aesthetically appealing. Rather than drawing an image, taking a photograph, or searching for a suitable stock image, it can be generated in a matter of seconds.

Instead of spending long periods of time writing copy, company policies, or other types of written communications, the content can be generated almost instantly, although it usually requires human editing for a finishing touch. Figure 8-1 is an example of AI-generated content used in a visual communication—showcasing a photorealistic image and a plant care guide for a fictional nursery.

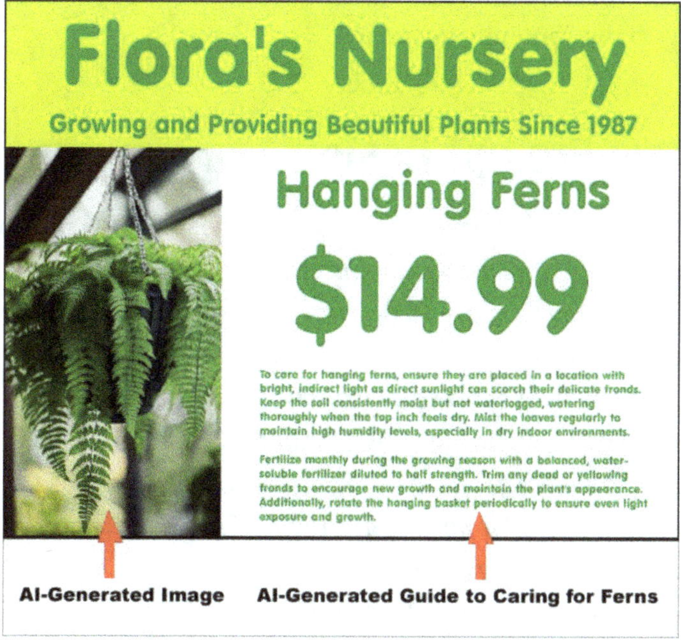

Figure 8-1. *An example of incorporating AI-generated content into a visual communication piece*

A Brief Introduction to ChatGPT

ChatGPT is an AI chatbot available in several iterations developed by OpenAI. ChatGPT-3.5 can be used for free but requires setting up an account with OpenAI. While ChatGPT-3.5 has no knowledge of events after September 2021, it is still a very useful tool for content generation. GPT-4 is available through the ChatGPT Plus subscription plan, which costs $20 per month for individuals. To use ChatGPT, simply create an account with OpenAI by visiting the site at `https://openai.com/`. We'll now look at several areas in which ChatGPT can be beneficial and how to maximize the quality of the content it generates.

Effective Prompt Design and Tuning

The quality of the output desired depends on clear and detailed prompts, a practice referred to as *prompt engineering*. When the result isn't quite adequate, adjusting the prompt (known as *prompt tuning*) will usually produce improved output.

Here's an example of how an owner of a plant nursery might a design a prompt to generate a guide to caring for potted ferns:

Prompt: *Generate a one paragraph guide to caring for potted ferns.*

Response: *Caring for potted ferns requires maintaining the right balance of light, water, and humidity. Place your fern in indirect light, as direct sunlight can scorch its delicate fronds. Water the plant regularly to keep the soil consistently moist but not waterlogged; the soil should be well-draining to prevent root rot. Ferns thrive in high humidity, so misting the leaves regularly or placing the pot on a tray filled with pebbles and water can help maintain the necessary moisture levels. Avoid drafts and sudden temperature changes, and use a balanced, water-soluble fertilizer every few months to support healthy growth.*

ChatGPT generated a good general guide to caring for potted ferns, but if your nursery is located in the Deep South, which experiences more extreme summer heat, inputting a more specific prompt (prompt tuning) will help produce a revised response as shown here:

Prompt: *Generate a one paragraph guide to caring for potted ferns in the Deep South region of the USA.*

Response: *Caring for potted ferns in the Deep South region of the USA involves managing the high heat and humidity typical of this area. Place your ferns in a location with bright, indirect light to avoid scorching the delicate fronds. Keep the soil consistently moist, but ensure it is well-draining to prevent root rot. High humidity is essential for fern health; mist the plants regularly or use a humidity tray filled with water and pebbles. During the peak summer heat, consider bringing your ferns indoors or placing them in a shaded area to protect them from extreme temperatures. Fertilize every 2-3 months with a balanced, water-soluble fertilizer to support healthy growth. Regularly check for pests and ensure proper air circulation to keep your ferns thriving.*

Sources:

- *Gardening Know How* (`https://www.gardeningknowhow.com`
- *Better Homes & Gardens* (`https://www.bhg.com`)
- *The Spruce* (`https://www.thespruce.com`)

We can see how tuning the prompt resulted in a better tailored response. It is important to bear in mind ChatGPT can generate inaccurate information (sometimes known as AI hallucinations); it's important to double-check the information that is produced. One tactic that can help reduce errors (although not foolproof) is to begin each prompt with the sentence "Make sure the content that will be generated is completely accurate." It may still be necessary to cross-reference the generated content with subject matter experts.

Brainstorming Using ChatGPT

ChatGPT can be a valuable resource to aid in generating creative ideas to help market, enhance, or troubleshoot your business. Let's suppose the fictional company *Midtown Cycle Shop* mentioned in Chapter 2 has recently opened for business, and the owner is seeking ways to introduce the company and engage with the local community. Here's an example of how ChatGPT can be utilized:

Prompt: *I am the proprietor of Midtown Cycle Shop, a new store that recently opened in a growing small city that has a river walk, several bike trails, and a couple of college campuses. Generate 10 ideas my company can use for community engagement to raise awareness of our new bicycle store, and have a Grand Opening.*

Response: *Congratulations on the grand opening of Midtown Cycle Shop! Here are ten creative ideas to engage the community and elevate awareness of your new establishment:*

1. *River Ride Rally: Organize a celebratory group bike ride along the scenic river walk, inviting cyclists of all ages and skill levels to join. Conclude the ride at Midtown Cycle Shop, where participants can enjoy refreshments, music, and exclusive discounts on merchandise.*

2. *Trailblazer Treasure Hunt: Host a community-wide scavenger hunt along the city's bike trails, with clues leading participants to hidden checkpoints and landmarks. Offer enticing prizes donated by local businesses, including gift vouchers or premium cycling gear available at Midtown Cycle Shop.*

3. *Campus Cruiser Carnival: Partner with nearby college campuses to host a lively carnival-style event featuring bike-themed games, competitions, and interactive workshops. Showcase your store's offerings with a dedicated booth offering special discounts and promotions for students and faculty.*

4. *Pedal-Powered Parade: Lead a colorful procession through the city streets, inviting cyclists to decorate their bikes in vibrant themes and costumes. Drum up excitement by offering prizes for the most creative and eye-catching bike designs. The parade can culminate at Midtown Cycle Shop with live music, food trucks, and festivities.*

5. *Pedestrian Plaza Pop-Up: Transform a bustling pedestrian area into a temporary pop-up market showcasing Midtown Cycle Shop's merchandise and services. Set up interactive displays, offer complimentary bike fittings, and provide live demonstrations of bike maintenance techniques to engage passersby.*

6. *Community Mural Project: Collaborate with local artists and community members to create a large-scale mural celebrating cycling culture and the city's unique landmarks. Host a public unveiling ceremony at Midtown Cycle Shop, inviting the community to admire the artwork and enjoy refreshments.*

7. *Bike Swap & Trade Event: Organize a bike swap event where cyclists can buy, sell, or trade bikes and accessories. Encourage participants to bring their pre-loved gear for exchange, and offer exclusive discounts on new purchases at Midtown Cycle Shop for attendees.*

8. *Pedal-Powered Film Night: Host an outdoor movie screening in a nearby park or outdoor venue, featuring classic cycling-themed films and documentaries. Provide blankets and popcorn for attendees, and promote your store's grand opening with special offers and giveaways during the event.*

9. *Cycle Commuter Challenge: Launch a friendly competition to encourage residents to commute by bike for a week. Offer incentives such as raffle prizes or gift certificates to Midtown Cycle Shop for participants who log the most miles or share their cycling experiences on social media using a designated hashtag.*

10. *Bike Donation Drive: Give back to the community by organizing a bike donation drive to support local charities or youth programs. Invite residents to donate gently used bikes at Midtown Cycle Shop and offer discounts on new purchases as a token of appreciation for their generosity.*

These engaging activities will not only raise awareness of your new store but also foster a sense of camaraderie and excitement within the community. Best of luck with your grand opening festivities!

As we can see, ChatGPT produced ten ideas, but let's suppose only a few are useful. For example, if you'd prefer to conduct in-store events only, then your prompt could be refined so it will generate responses that fit within the stated parameters. ChatGPT can also help you develop long-term marketing plans, plan seasonal promotions, etc.

Another area in which ChatGPT can help brainstorm is creating company procedure guides and other training materials (often lacking in the small, independent retail sector). In the past, creating a procedure guide to help onboard new employees was time-consuming, and it wasn't often a high priority. Now, generating procedure guides and other training materials can be done almost instantly. Here's an example of an onboarding guide Midtown Cycle Shop can create for distribution to new employees:

Prompt: *I've just opened Midtown Cycle Shop, a bicycle shop that sells new and used bikes. We also sell accessories, as well as service and repair bicycles. Our company employees 10 people on average. I want to minimize the turnover rate many small retailers experience. Generate an onboarding guide that will help thoroughly train employees, and help retain them long term. Include financial incentives for each milestone achieved.*

Response: *Creating a comprehensive onboarding guide is crucial for effectively training employees and fostering long-term retention. Here's a structured onboarding guide for Midtown Cycle Shop, incorporating training modules and financial incentives for employee milestones:*

Midtown Cycle Shop Onboarding Guide

Welcome to the Team!

Welcome aboard to Midtown Cycle Shop! We're excited to have you join our team and contribute to our mission of providing exceptional service and expertise to our customers. This onboarding guide is designed to help you get up to speed with our company, products, and processes, and to support your growth and success as a valued member of our team.

1. ***Company Overview***

    - *Provide an overview of Midtown Cycle Shop, including our history, mission, and values.*

    - *Introduce key team members and departments, and explain the roles and responsibilities within the organization.*

2. ***Product Training***

    - *Familiarize yourself with the products we offer, including new and used bikes, accessories, and service offerings.*
    - *Learn about the features and specifications of different bike models, and understand how to match customer needs with appropriate products.*
    - *Receive hands-on training in bike assembly, maintenance, and repair procedures.*

3. ***Customer Service Excellence***

    - *Understand the importance of providing excellent customer service and building positive relationships with customers.*
    - *Learn effective communication skills for interacting with customers both in-person and over the phone.*
    - *Practice handling common customer inquiries, issues, and complaints with empathy and professionalism.*

4. ***Sales Techniques***

    - *Learn effective sales techniques for promoting products and services, including upselling and cross-selling strategies.*
    - *Understand the sales process from greeting customers to closing sales, and practice active listening and problem-solving skills.*
    - *Receive training on our point-of-sale (POS) system and how to process transactions accurately and efficiently.*

5. ***Safety and Compliance***

    - *Review safety protocols and procedures for working in the shop, including proper handling of tools and equipment, and safe lifting techniques.*
    - *Understand compliance requirements related to bike sales, service, and repairs, including warranty policies and industry regulations.*

6. ***Professional Development***

    - *Set personalized goals and objectives for your professional development and career growth within Midtown Cycle Shop.*
    - *Participate in ongoing training and skill development opportunities, such as workshops, seminars, and online courses.*
    - *Take advantage of mentorship and coaching opportunities with experienced team members to enhance your skills and knowledge.*

Financial Incentives for Milestones Achieved

To recognize and reward your contributions and achievements, Midtown Cycle Shop offers the following financial incentives for reaching key milestones:

- ***Completion of Onboarding Training:*** *Receive a one-time bonus upon successful completion of the onboarding training program.*
- ***Sales Performance Bonuses:*** *Earn bonuses based on sales performance targets, such as achieving monthly sales goals or upselling service packages.*

- ***Customer Satisfaction Incentives:*** *Receive incentives based on positive customer feedback and satisfaction ratings.*
- ***Longevity Rewards:*** *Earn additional bonuses or perks for reaching milestone anniversaries with Midtown Cycle Shop, such as one year, three years, and five years of service.*

By implementing this comprehensive onboarding guide and offering financial incentives for employee milestones, Midtown Cycle Shop can effectively train and retain employees, fostering a positive and motivated team environment.

The generated content serves as the framework upon which a comprehensive employee onboarding guide can be built. The text can be copied and pasted from ChatGPT into a word processing application such as Microsoft Word, LibreOffice (a free, open source alternative to Word), or another similar program. It can then be further formatted, edited, and refined.

For a finishing touch, a professional quality cover page can be designed for the document. The example shown in Figure 8-2 was created using Paint.NET (it can be done using GIMP as well). Notice it follows the same color scheme, employs the same graphical element, and uses the same typeface family for the company name as the business card design featured in Chapter 2, maintaining consistent branding.

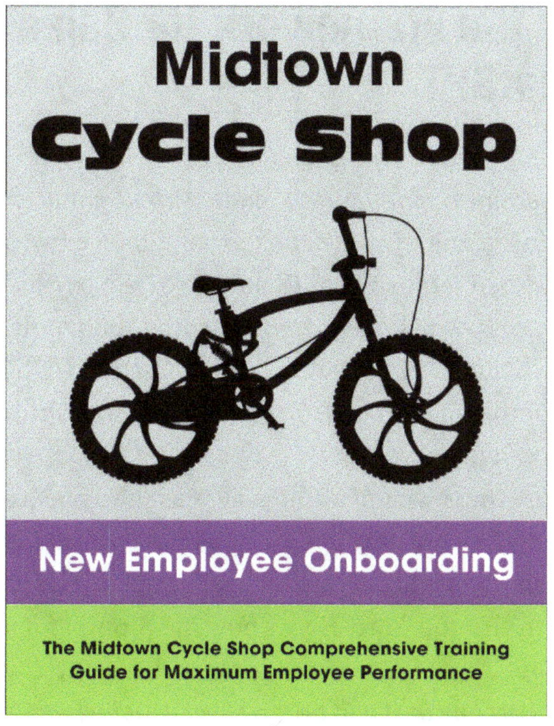

Figure 8-2. *An example of cover page design for adding a professional touch to the company's guide for onboarding new employees*

These are examples of using ChatGPT for brainstorming. It can generate responses that can be edited and customized for the unique needs of any business. It's easy to see how valuable this practice can be in getting any new business off to a good start or improve operations in well-established businesses.

Generate the Framework for Sales Copy Using ChatGPT

Creating sales copy is usually handled by *copywriters,* who are trained to write persuasively to motivate the reader to take some type of action (which is usually buying a product or service). In recent years, companies have begun to use AI tools such as ChatGPT to help streamline the copywriting process, which has raised concerns about potentially displacing copywriters. While the content generated by ChatGPT may be mediocre compared to that of an experienced copywriter, it can be improved with careful editing.

Let's suppose the owner of Midtown Cycle Shop plans on creating a flyer announcing they are now open for business, which can be displayed around town. The flyer will contain two paragraphs of copy designed to entice readers to visit the store. Here's how the prompt might read:

Prompt: *You, ChatGPT, are an expert copywriter. I'd like you to write two paragraphs of copy that will be on a flyer, in which many copies will be displayed around town. The copy should be written in a way to motivate readers to visit the store. We are offering 15% off of select bicycles and accessories. The staff at Midtown Cycle Shop is experienced, and we undergo continuous training to keep abreast of the latest in cycling . Our goal is to provide the best quality and value to our customers possible.*

Response: ***Gear Up for Adventure at Midtown Cycle Shop!***

Embark on your cycling journey with unbeatable savings! Discover the thrill of the ride with 15% off select bicycles and accessories at Midtown Cycle Shop. Whether you're a seasoned cyclist or just starting out, our knowledgeable staff is here to guide you every pedal of the way. With years of experience and ongoing training, we're dedicated to staying ahead of the curve, ensuring you receive top-notch service and expertise.

At Midtown Cycle Shop, excellence is our standard. We're committed to providing you with the highest quality products and the best value, making your cycling experience truly unforgettable. Visit us today and let us help you find the perfect gear to fuel your passion for adventure on two wheels. Don't miss out on this exclusive offer - pedal into savings and join the Midtown Cycle Shop family today!

The content it produced is a viable framework that could be used as is; more often than not, some degree of editing will be required.

Critique and Evaluate Designs Using ChatGPT Plus

ChatGPT Plus (the paid version) is capable of analyzing attachments such as images, PDFs, and other types of content. It can be especially useful for providing feedback and suggestions for improving your designs. Figure 8-3 displays the thumbnail of a design uploaded for the AI system to analyze while prompting it to provide feedback on the design's strengths and areas that can be improved.

Figure 8-3. *The thumbnail of a design uploaded for ChatGPT Plus to scan and provide feedback on its strengths and areas for improvement based on the prompt*

In addition to providing feedback and suggestions for improving your design, ChatGPT Plus can also provide a visual reference (called a *wireframe*) to assist in the placement of each element of your design.

When using ChatGPT Plus to make suggestions for improvements, simply add the words "Include wireframe reference." as the last sentence of the prompt, and it will produce a text- and character-based graphical representation, displaying its suggested placement of elements (Figure 8-4).

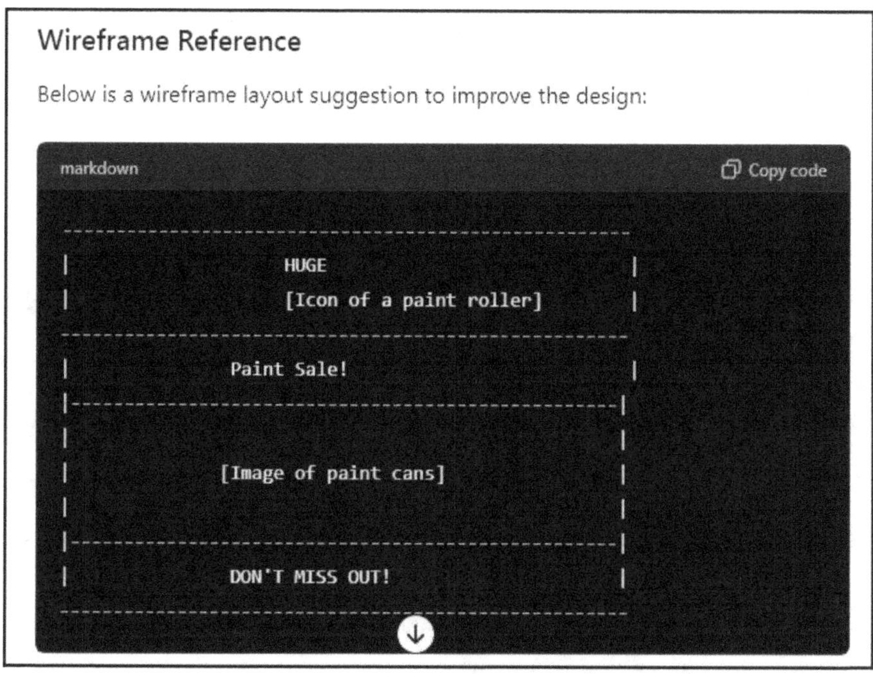

Figure 8-4. *A wireframe is useful for showing suggested placement of graphical elements in your design*

AI Image and Video Generators

In this section, we'll touch on AI image and video generation resources for aiding small businesses in creating visual content. While there seems to be some overall mixed sentiment about using AI-generated images and video (some people feel it's too inauthentic), the fact is that AI can help expedite the process of creating visual communications. Of course, there are ethical considerations, which we'll touch on a little later.

Let's suppose that the owner of Midtown Cycle Shop wants to create a brochure that can be distributed to prospective customers. He'd like to include an image of several cyclists riding mountain bikes along a scenic route but has been unable to find a suitable stock image. Using an AI image generator can help produce one to suit his needs. Using Pixlr's AI Image Generator (which we covered briefly in Chapter 6), entering the prompt "group of cyclists riding mountain bikes on a scenic trail" in the *Generate* field, four versions of the requested image are produced as depicted in Figure 8-5.

Figure 8-5. *Four versions of an image generated in Pixlr's AI Image Generator*

There are a number of AI image and video generators available to assist small business owners in creating visual content. This chapter will touch on a couple of them.

DALL-E 3

DALL-E 3 is OpenAI's image generator. Now in its third version, it boasts improved capabilities such as better understanding of nuanced prompts, resulting in higher-quality outputs. Currently, DALL-E 3 can be accessed on OpenAI's subscription platform. However, platforms such as *Microsoft Designer* and *Bing Image Creator* integrate DALL-E 3, so it can be tried out at no cost (although there may be some limitations). Figure 8-6 shows an example of four versions of cyclists generated by DALL-E 3 in Microsoft Designer, using the same prompt as that in Pixlr AI Image Creator.

Figure 8-6. *Four versions of an image generated in Microsoft Designer, powered by DALL-E 3*

Another example shown in Figure 8-7 shows four versions of a bicycle shop employee performing a repair, which was also generated by DALL-E 3 in Microsoft Designer.

Figure 8-7. *Four versions of an image generated in Microsoft Designer, powered by DALL-E 3*

If you're signed in to a personal Microsoft account, you're allotted 15 *boosts* per day; boosts allow you to generate images more quickly. If you run out of boosts, it takes longer to generate images; boosts will replenish the next day. Subscribers to *Microsoft Copilot Pro* receive 100 boosts per day.

For those with ChatGPT Plus or Enterprise plans, DALL-E 3 can integrate with ChatGPT. This allows the user to generate images while conversing with ChatGPT, thereby increasing work efficiency.

To learn more about DALL-E 3, visit the web page here: `https://openai.com/index/dall-e-3/`.

Generating Content with Runway

Runway is a popular resource for generating images, video, audio, and 3D. It also offers tools such as *Text to Speech* for adding voice over dialogue to video. *Lip Sync* can be used to animate lip movement in still characters, synchronizing it with spoken dialogue. Images generated in Runway can also be edited in various ways. One such feature is the *Motion Brush Tool,* which allows you to animate selected areas of a still image; you can draw on specific areas and adjust the direction and intensity of the motion.

Here are some of the features that are available in Runway:

- **Text to-Image:** Generates images by inputting descriptive text-based prompts
- **Text to Video:** Generates video (maximum length of 18 seconds) by inputting descriptive text-based prompts
- **Image to Video:** Generates video from a still image
- **Video to Video:** Generates new visual content from existing videos
- **Image to Image:** Transforms existing images using a text-based prompt

  Runway also offers tools for generating audio using text prompts, cleaning audio by removing unwanted background noises, and much more.

Runway can be tried out at no cost by setting up an account. You'll have access to a limited number of generative models. Figure 8-8 depicts an image that was created using Runway's *Text to Image* tool.

Figure 8-8. *This example was created by using Runway's Text-to-Image tool*

Note After you generate AI-based images for a while, you'll notice that the text (such as the sign in this example) is usually distorted or misspelled. This is because the AI model is designed to generate image content and not trained specifically for rendering text. If the text is a necessary element in the generated image, Paint.NET or GIMP can be used to manually edit or replace the text.

To learn more about Runway and try it out, visit `https://runwayml.com/`.

Ethical Considerations

Generative AI is a powerful resource that can aid business owners of all kinds, but it's important to use it wisely and responsibly. There are legitimate concerns that as AI advances, there will be a point that generated content will be indistinguishable from reality. This can open the door to misuse, creating content that's deceptive or harmful.

As we've seen in this chapter, AI-generated content can be both expedient and economical; in short, it can be a game-changer for small business owners. Of course, it's important to maintain transparency when incorporating it into your visual communications.

Let's take for example the sign that was designed for the fictional plant nursery; it has an AI-generated image of a potted fern. Customers seeing this sign might think it's an actual photograph. In addition, the plant care guide was also AI generated. The owner of the nursery can likely verify the accuracy, but a less experienced employee might not be able to.

My recommendation is placing a small disclaimer in visual communications containing AI-generated content for transparency. This can help mitigate a sense of customer mistrust if it's discovered the content wasn't human generated. Figure 8-9 demonstrates how such a disclaimer can be used. It reads: "Disclaimer: This image and guide were generated using AI technology. Actual product appearance may differ slightly from the image. For best results, please verify care information with additional resources."

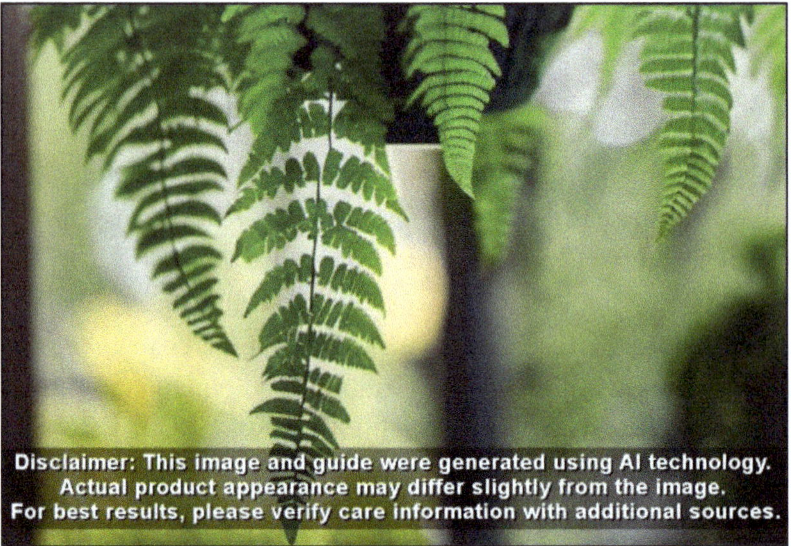

Figure 8-9. *Placing a disclaimer on visual communications containing AI-generated content helps maintain transparency*

Another thing to consider is this—who owns the copyright to the content you generate using AI? This topic still seems to be in question to some degree. Generative AI draws on data that's in cyberspace, books, and other sources. The terms of use may differ from platform to another. For example, most platforms state that any image you generate can be used for commercial purposes. However, one may claim ownership to the image; this means you can use it in your visual communications, but it technically belongs to the AI platform that generated it.

It's important to read the terms of use and legal aspects of any generative AI platform you use.

Summary

In this chapter, we explored some of the benefits (and concerns) using generative AI. Here's what was covered:

- A brief introduction to generative AI
- A brief introduction to ChatGPT (this discussed prompt design, brainstorming, generating written content, and evaluating designs using ChatGPT)
- AI image and video generators (which touched on DALL-E 3 and Runway)
- Ethical considerations

In the next chapter, we'll look at ways to economize on creating large format visuals, such as posters and graphics for vehicles.

CHAPTER 9

Large Format and Vehicle Graphics

In this chapter, we'll explore ways to cut costs in large format printing and vehicle graphics. Here's what we'll cover:

- Large format printers
- Resources for printing posters
  - Getting the most from your posters
- Budget-friendly tips for utilizing vehicle graphics
  - Cut vinyl letters and decals
  - Vehicle magnets
- Summary

Large Format Printers

Many, if not most, small business printing needs are satisfied with an ordinary inkjet, copier, or laser printer that prints letter size (8.5" × 11") or legal size (8.5" × 14") paper. If your business requires printing larger format documents on a regular basis, you'll need to weigh whether it's more cost-effective to invest in a large format printer or use a printing service.

P. Whitt, *Cost-Effective Graphic Solutions for Small Businesses*, Apress Pocket Guides,
https://doi.org/10.1007/979-8-8688-1192-0_9

For the purposes of this chapter, I'll refer to anything larger than legal size as "large format," although technically the next size up is 11" × 17", which is tabloid size.

For a small retailer that prints a lot of in-store signage, 11" × 17" would be a good choice for placing in the windows for pedestrians to see more easily when passing by (but not be too large to obstruct the window or door too much). These are also a good choice for printing bifold or trifold brochures or company communications requiring 11" × 17" paper.

Tabloid inkjet printers can range from around $200 for a low-end model up to around $1000 for a higher-end model capable of producing excellent quality prints. Laser printers are usually more expensive, ranging from roughly $500 to $2000.

The next size up is 13" × 19", which is commonly known as "Super B" or "Super A3." This size is good for large art or photographic prints, as well as small posters. Inkjet models range from around $230 to $1200; laser models can range from around $1000 to $2500. Printers capable of larger sizes can cost up to $10,000 or more, depending on the size and purpose.

If you shop for a large format printer, consider a good used model. Check online markets such as eBay, or contact local office supply stores to see if they might have one available. It is a bit of a risk, however. It could save you a lot of money at the outset, but the potential downside is there might not be a warranty available.

The costs of paper and ink (or toner, if using a laser printer) are also factors to consider when shopping for a printer. These sundries tend to be rather costly; 13" × 19" paper can start at $30 (per pack of 50 sheets). Some inkjet printers utilize large ink capacity reservoirs; these models are more expensive but are more economical in the long run because the ink supply lasts much longer.

Resources for Printing Posters

If you'd rather opt to have your posters and other large format visuals printed by a service, there are numerous online services available, such as UPrinting or Vistaprint. You can upload an existing design or design your poster using the service's online tools. Once you're satisfied with the design, just place your order. 16" × 20" posters (printed on one side) average about $13 each.

These services can print business cards, brochures, and a wide array of other business communications.

To learn more about UPrinting, visit `https://www.uprinting.com/`.

To learn more about Vistaprint, visit `https://www.vistaprint.com/`.

Getting the Most from Your Posters

When I was an advertising manager for a medium-sized home center back in the early 1990s, we frequently had sales and promotions on house and wall paint. Even though the promotional posters were provided by the paint supplier that sponsored the promotion, we usually had to discard them after the sale because they were designed for a temporary period, so they weren't usable after the promotion.

However, on occasion, we received some that were "generic" enough that we would save them when the sale ended and reuse them for our own in-store sales. Figure 9-1 shows an example of a paint sale poster that could be reused throughout the year. It can last a long time if stored properly between promotions.

Figure 9-1. *A generic poster can be reused when stored properly between promotions*

Posters will eventually wear out and fade over time, but the longer you keep and reuse them, the more money you can save. Here are a few tips to help you preserve them as long as possible.

- Use inexpensive poster board to reinforce it as shown in Figure 9-2; use spray adhesive to affix it to the poster board; this will help add longer life. Foam core board would add more rigidity but is more expensive.

Figure 9-2. *Use inexpensive poster board to add reinforcement*

- If your budget allows, laminate your posters; this will help them last much longer.
- An alternative to laminating the entire poster is to use clear, 2-inch-wide clear packing tape and laminate the edges (Figure 9-3).

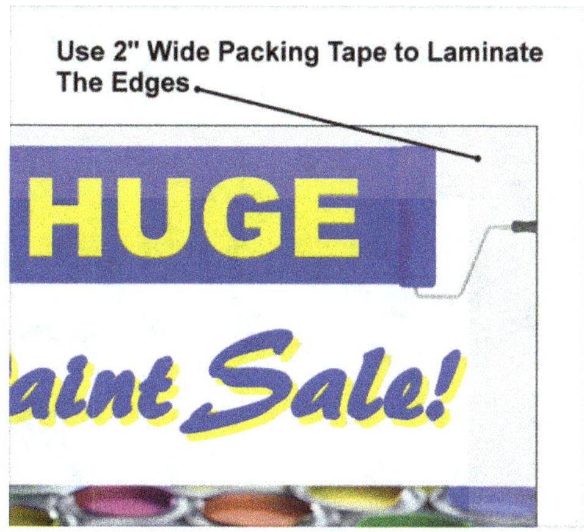

Figure 9-3. *An alternative to laminating the entire poster is to use 2-inch-wide packing tape to laminate the edges*

- If your posters are displayed in areas that receive sunlight, consider purchasing an aerosol clear coat spray to help protect it from damaging ultraviolet rays.

Budget-Friendly Tips for Utilizing Vehicle Graphics

Using signs and graphics on company vehicles is a great way to market your business; this can be especially helpful to freelancers or solopreneurs with limited budgets. Let's look at a few low-cost options to help turn your vehicle into a "rolling billboard."

Cut Vinyl Letters and Decals

This option is simply cutting letters and shapes from vinyl sheets with an adhesive back that are placed on vehicle windows (or on the body). Figure 9-4 shows an example of basic cut vinyl letters on the window of a fictional company van that offers pool services.

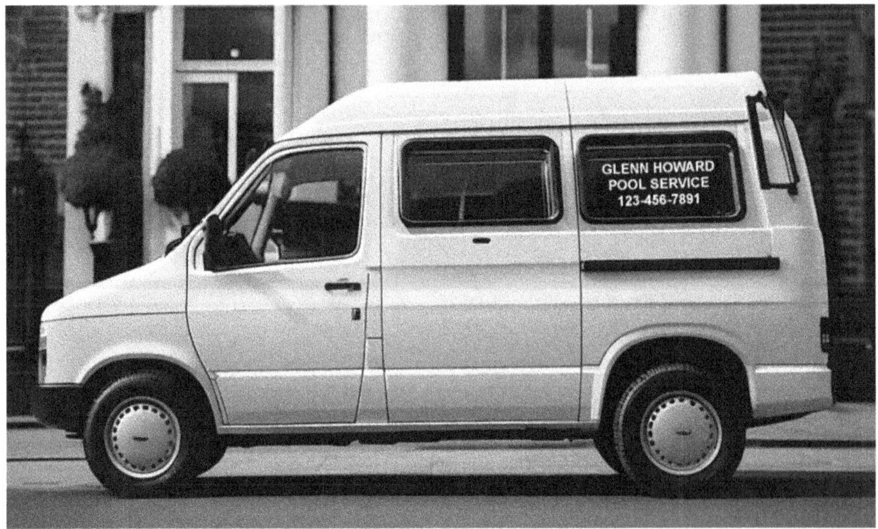

Figure 9-4. *Cut vinyl letters are a basic, inexpensive way of using your vehicle to market your company*

If you prefer to do it yourself, sheets of cut vinyl letters are available at hardware stores and home centers for around $10 per pack. Depending on how many letters are required, it may take multiple packs.

Opting for a sign company to do it for you will be more expensive, but the results will look more polished and professional; using premium material would also be more weather resistant and last longer. Depending on what you have put on your vehicle, the cost could range from $50 to $150.

Cut vinyl can also be cut into decals to form graphics and logos. Figure 9-5 shows an example of a simple vinyl decal with cut letters and a simple shape depicting water in a pool.

Figure 9-5. *Vinyl can be cut into decals forming graphics and logos*

Depending on the complexity of the graphics, vehicle area coverage, and number of colors, the cost can range from $50 to $500.

Vehicle Magnets

Vehicle magnets are another inexpensive option. These can be purchased from Vistaprint and other online markets. One advantage magnets offer is that they are removable; if you use your personal vehicle for business purposes, there may be time you'll want to remove it.

Magnets are a good option because you can design your own graphics or use a predesigned template. Figure 9-6 shows an example of how a magnetic sign would look on our fictional company van.

Figure 9-6. *Magnetic signs are another inexpensive option that can be removed when needed*

Magnets for vehicles can range from $30 to $100 each. To help them look their best (and to protect your vehicle's finish), they should be removed and cleaned regularly to remove dirt and grit from between the back of the magnet and the surface of the vehicle.

Vehicle wraps and custom painted graphics are very attention getting (Figure 9-7); they can cover part or all of the vehicle but can cost thousands of dollars. If you're an upstart or just on a budget, this could be something to work toward as your business gets more established.

Figure 9-7. *Custom wraps or painted graphics are very noticeable but can cost thousands*

Summary

We learned some about large format printers, as well as graphics for vehicles. Here's what was covered:

- Large format printers
- Resources for printing posters
    - Getting the most from your posters
- Budget-friendly tips for utilizing vehicle graphics
    - Cut vinyl letters and decals
    - Vehicle magnets

In the last chapter, we'll look at ways your company can create a branding culture.

PART IV

Employee Involvement

CHAPTER 10

Cultivating a Visual Branding Culture

It's evident that DIY design has become more common in recent years with the advent of platforms such as Canva, Pixlr, Marq, etc. Graphic design was once in the purview of specialists who were trained for many years in the graphic arts (and that is still true today), but now, the ability to create compelling visual designs is within the reach of nonprofessional designers.

In this chapter, we'll look at how a small business can involve its employees in the branding and visual content creation process. Here's what we'll look at:

- The importance of employee participation in visual branding
- Emphasizing the importance of branding
- Benefits of engaging employees in visual branding efforts
- Encouraging creativity and contribution
- Establishing guidelines for consistency
- Implementing incentive programs for employee contributions
- Recognizing outstanding efforts in visual branding
- Summary

P. Whitt, *Cost-Effective Graphic Solutions for Small Businesses*, Apress Pocket Guides,
https://doi.org/10.1007/979-8-8688-1192-0_10

The Importance of Employee Participation in Visual Branding

Branding is what creates a company's unique and recognizable identity. While the logo and color scheme are important components in a company's branding, it's also about the unique products and customer service that makes it stand out from the competition. Involving employees in the company's branding allows them to bring unique perspectives and ideas and helps them better understand the company's mission and more invested in the company's success (Figure 10-1).

Figure 10-1. *Involving employees in the branding process helps bring unique perspectives and ideas to the table and reinforces the company's mission. (Image courtesy of Pexels)*

Emphasizing the Importance of Branding

A well-defined brand identity can help a small business set themselves apart from competitors (especially larger companies with large marketing budgets) and build a loyal customer base. Branding should encompass every avenue a customer (or prospective customer) has with the business; this includes store layout for small retailers, social media posts, employee uniforms, promotional materials, etc.

As an example, a small independent hardware store can differentiate itself from a big box store by offering personalized customer service, expert advice from a knowledgeable staff, specialized products, promotions, customer loyalty programs, and community involvement. Smaller hardware companies offering services that aren't available at larger box stores can help them stand out in customers' minds (Figure 10-2).

Figure 10-2. *By offering services unavailable at larger box stores, a smaller hardware store can reinforce its brand in customers' minds*

The Benefits of Engaging Employees in Visual Branding Efforts

Here are several benefits to consider in involving your employees in the company's visual branding efforts:

1. **Diverse Perspectives:** Employees with varying job roles and backgrounds can help provide unique insights that contribute to more innovative and appealing visual content. As an example, a produce

manager from a local grocery market could be involved in the design of signage announcing the arrival of a new product (Figure 10-3).

Figure 10-3. *A produce manager of a local grocery market could be involved in creating signage announcing a new product*

2. **Increased Engagement:** When employees are involved in the branding process, they usually feel a sense of participation and pride in the company's success. This can help foster better employee performance and retention.

3. **Cost-Effectiveness:** By involving internal resources for visual content creation, you can reduce (or possibly eliminate) the need for an outside graphic designer or firm.

4. **Consistency:** When employees are involved in the branding and visual content creation process, they can better understand the importance of maintaining branding uniformity in marketing materials.

Encouraging Creativity and Contribution

To encourage employee creativity, it's important to create an environment where employee ideas are welcome. Even though an idea might not be implemented, it can be recorded for possible use in the future. Being dismissive toward employees that are contributing ideas can be demoralizing; you may not yield useful results if that happens.

1. **Brainstorming Sessions:** Consider holding regular meetings for brainstorming sessions; you never know when a brilliant idea might emerge.

2. **Design Workshops:** If possible, consider holding workshops or training sessions on basic design principles and tools like Canva or Pixlr to help employees develop their skills. When time is limited, it could even be helpful to watch short tutorials on YouTube and trying out what they learn when business is slower and more time is available.

3. **Open Communication:** It's important for employees to feel that what they say matters; openly ridiculing someone's idea during a meeting or brainstorming session serves no useful purpose. Conversely, sarcastic or unprofessional remarks from employees that don't value the branding culture you seek to establish should not be tolerated. When the door to open communication is open, employees will usually participate in the process in a meaningful way.

Establishing Guidelines for Consistency

Even though employees can contribute greatly to a small company's creation of visual content, it's important to maintain consistency across all of visual elements. Establish clear guidelines that outline:

1. **Branding Standards:** If the company is still new and in the process of being firmly established, define the company's color scheme, logo design, typography, and other visual elements.
2. **Template Library:** Maintain a library of templates for flyers, business cards, brochures, and other marketing and visual communications. This can help maintain consistency and streamline the design process (no need to create a new one from scratch every time).
3. **Final Approval:** Have a process for approving final designs (this would usually be done by the owner or manager) before publication.

Implementing Incentive Programs for Employee Contributions

To establish a strong branding culture among your employees, consider implementing incentive programs:

1. **Recognition Programs:** Highlight outstanding contributions employees make in company meetings, newsletters, or other company publications/announcements.

2. **Competitions:** Organizing design completions can be a great way to help employees create outstanding work. Establish an impartial way to judge participants' work (such as a small panel).

3. **Professional Development:** If there are one or two employees that stand out in contributing to your branding efforts, consider fostering professional development. It could lead to a new, full-time position in your company, or it could be a regular part of their other duties. Consider providing opportunities for advanced design training to your employee(s).

Recognizing Outstanding Efforts in Visual Branding

When employees are making noteworthy contributions in your branding efforts, it's important to recognize and celebrate them. Here are a few ideas to consider:

1. **Employee of the Month:** Recognize and highlight employees who have made significant contributions to the company's branding efforts in an Employee of the Month program. This can be a great way to instill a sense of accomplishment in your employee.

2. **Spotlight Features:** Share success stories and showcase employee-created content on the company's website or social media platforms.

3. **Personal Acknowledgments:** Provide personalized thank-you notes, small gifts, or even monetary rewards for employees who have gone above and beyond.

As you can see, actively involving employees in your company's branding efforts can help create a more cohesive and vibrant organization. Employees who feel valued and that they are making a worthwhile contribution are generally happier and more productive (Figure 10-4).

Figure 10-4. *Involving employees in your company's branding efforts can help create a more productive and vibrant workplace. (Image courtesy of Pexels)*

Summary

In this chapter, we learned that employee involvement in your company's branding efforts can not only help reduce costs but can help foster a sense of pride and accomplishment among your employees. Here's what was covered:

- The importance of employee participation in visual branding

- Emphasizing the importance of branding
- Benefits of engaging employees in visual branding efforts
- Encouraging creativity and contribution
- Establishing guidelines for consistency
- Implementing incentive programs for employee contributions
- Recognizing outstanding efforts in visual branding

Thank you for taking some time to read this book, and hope you found it helpful in your quest for cost-effective visual content resources. Best wishes in your business endeavors!

PART V

Useful Learning Resources

CHAPTER 11

Useful Learning Resources

In this section, we'll look at a number of learning resources to help you get the most out of the free programs Paint.NET, GIMP, and FotoSketcher. There's also a book I'll discuss titled *Ogilvy on Advertising*. It's an old publication, but I believe it is still relevant today and a great resource if you can find a copy. Some of these resources are the ones I published with Apress over the past few years, but there are some other ones as well.

Here's what we'll cover:

- Paint.NET
    - *Practical Paint.NET*
    - Paint.NET Tutorials in Autodesk Instructables
- GIMP
    - *Practical Glimpse*
    - *GIMP for Absolute Beginners*
- FotoSketcher
    - Digital Art Creation Using FotoSketcher
- *Ogilvy on Advertising*

P. Whitt, *Cost-Effective Graphic Solutions for Small Businesses*, Apress Pocket Guides,
https://doi.org/10.1007/979-8-8688-1192-0_11

Paint.NET

As you discovered early on in this book, Paint.NET is a free, Windows-based program for image editing and creation. I provided a tutorial on creating a marketing piece, but if you'd like to go further with this program, here are a few resources for learning more.

Practical Paint.NET

This book was published in 2022 by Apress (Figure 11-1). It covers everything from downloading and installation to using plug-ins that enhance functionality. This book covers mainly photo editing techniques but also covers raster image creation.

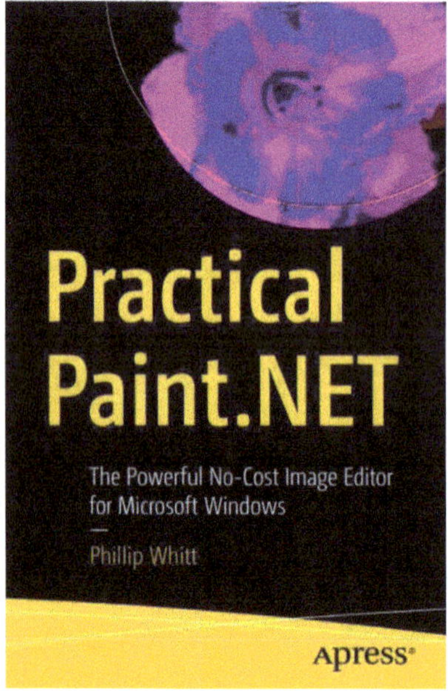

Figure 11-1. *Practical Paint.NET was published in 2022 and covers mainly photo editing but touches on raster graphic creation as well*

To learn more about this book, visit `https://link.springer.com/book/10.1007/978-1-4842-7283-1`.

Paint.NET Tutorials in Autodesk Instructables

This is a collection of various Paint.NET tutorials by various contributors. This is handy resource to learn how to perform a wide variety of tasks using Paint.NET. To learn more, visit `https://www.instructables.com/search/?q=paint.net&projects=all`.

GIMP

We covered this powerful program earlier in this book. GIMP is a popular alternative to Adobe Photoshop but has a steep learning curve for beginners. Here are several learning resources for this image editing powerhouse.

Practical Glimpse

Although it's no longer being developed or maintained, *Glimpse* was a fork of GIMP. Some of the developers splintered into their own group and developed this program, which is virtually identical to GIMP. Although *Glimpse* is no longer available, this Apress publication from 2020 (Figure 11-2) is completely applicable to GIMP 2.10 and higher.

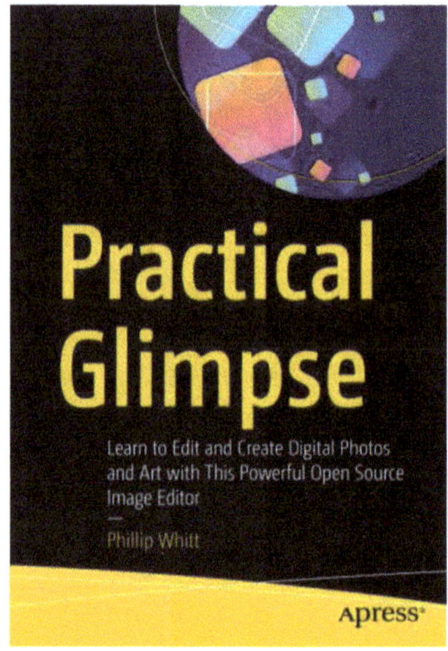

Figure 11-2. *Practical Glimpse was published in 2020 and applicable to GIMP*

To learn more about this book, visit `https://link.springer.com/book/10.1007/978-1-4842-6327-3`.

GIMP for Absolute Beginners

Authored by Jan Smith and Roman Joost, this is an older Apress publication 2012 (Figure 11-3); it can still be useful for helping new users get up and running with GIMP. It was written for GIMP 2.8, but the majority of the information still applies.

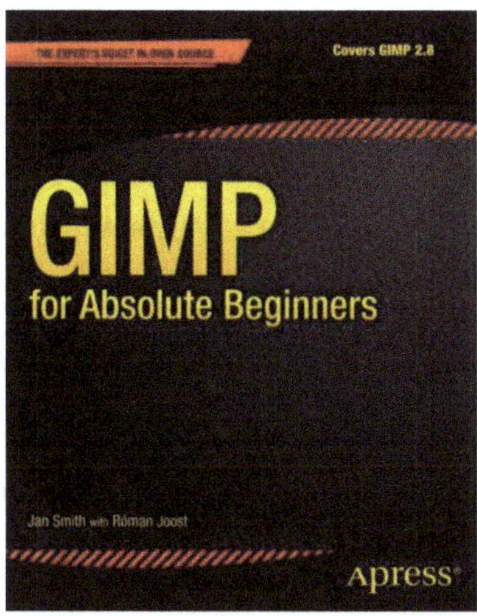

Figure 11-3. *GIMP for Absolute Beginners was published in 2012 but is still useful today*

To learn more about this book, visit `https://link.springer.com/book/10.1007/978-1-4302-3169-1`.

FotoSketcher

FotoSketcher is an easy-to-use Windows-based program for turning photos into digital art. The video course *Digital Art Creation Using FotoSketcher* (published by Apress in 2022) is available through the publisher's subscription program; this course takes a thorough look at what can be accomplished with this program.

To learn more, visit `https://link.springer.com/video/10.1007/978-1-4842-8284-7`.

Ogilvy on Advertising

This book by the late David Ogilvy is widely considered an essential read for professionals in creative fields like marketing and advertising. David Ogilvy, often hailed as "the father of advertising," founded his agency, Ogilvy & Mather, in 1948.

Though *Ogilvy on Advertising* was first published in 1983, much of its content remains highly relevant today. The book focuses primarily on print advertising and provides valuable insights into the principles of effective advertising. Ogilvy explores the key elements that make advertisements successful, offering timeless advice that continues to resonate in the industry.

There are still copies of this book available at online markets such as eBay, Amazon, and Thriftbooks.com.

GPSR Compliance
The European Union's (EU) General Product Safety Regulation (GPSR) is a set of rules that requires consumer products to be safe and our obligations to ensure this.

If you have any concerns about our products, you can contact us on

ProductSafety@springernature.com

In case Publisher is established outside the EU, the EU authorized representative is:

Springer Nature Customer Service Center GmbH
Europaplatz 3
69115 Heidelberg, Germany

www.ingramcontent.com/pod-product-compliance
Lightning Source LLC
LaVergne TN
LVHW051639050326
832903LV00022B/819

9798868811913